THE 100 one hundred greatest
Golfers

THE 100 one hundred greatest Golfers

PETER COSSINS

WITH A FOREWORD BY
SAM TORRANCE

generation
PUBLICATIONS

Peter Cossins is the editor in chief of the golf sites on the Rivals Europe internet sports network,
the largest network of fan sites on the web

"For Elaine and the CosDons"

Designed by Robert Kelland

GENERATION PUBLICATIONS

Editor: Phil McNeill
Publications Manager: Eve Cossins
Researcher: Mark Crossland
Publishers: David Crowe and Mark Peacock

With thanks to Nick Edmund, Mike Richards and Adrian Waddington;
and to Lara Piercy and Rob Brown at Colour Systems

Special thanks to Sam Torrance

First published in Great Britain in 2000 by Generation Publications
9 Holyrood Street, London SE1 2EL
020 7403 0364
genpub@btinternet.com

A catalogue record for this title is available from the British Library

ISBN 1 903009 31 6

Production by Mike Powell & Associates (01494 676891)
Origination by Colour Systems Ltd, London
Printed in Slovenia by arrangement with Korotan-Ljubljana d.o.o.

The photographs in the book are from Allsport, with thanks to Rob Harborne and Andy Redington,
and Phil Burnham-Richards at Hulton Getty;
from Corbis, with thanks to Helen Dobson;
and from Michael Hobbs

....

Page 1: Seve and Ollie, Ryder Cup, Kiawah Island, 1991
Page 2: Colin Montgomerie, Dubai Desert Classic, Dubai Creek GC, 1999
Page 3: Jimmy Demaret and Ben Hogan share a glass of milk, 1940

Contents

• Foreword •

by Sam Torrance

Writing the foreword for a book like this sure could make a guy feel his age! Looking down the list of The 100 Greatest Golfers, I was amazed to discover that I've played against no fewer than 57 of them. My 30 years in professional golf have been a privilege and a pleasure, and Peter Cossins' book brings back a flood of memories.

Once I started to compile my own Top Ten, I soon found it was an impossible job. Still, here goes...

Jack Nicklaus has to be No1 simply because of his astounding record – not just the 18 Majors, but all the seconds and thirds, which no one else could match.

I rank Ben Hogan equal with Jack because he was probably the greatest ball-striker that ever lived. If it hadn't been for the car crash in 1948 that restricted Hogan's career, he might even have surpassed Nicklaus.

Some people might be surprised to see Lee Trevino at No5, but Lee was the greatest shot-maker I ever played with. He could do almost anything with the ball, and he was such fun to be around.

Henry Cotton was a personal hero. I was Rookie Of The Year in 1972, and my prize was to spend two weeks with Henry Cotton. I played with him nearly every day. There I was, in my first year on the Tour, learning from this amazing champion who had won three Opens. He was in his sixties, while I was just 17, but it was an unforgettable experience.

There's no Tiger Woods in my list because at 24, he's simply too young. But in five years' time I expect Tiger to be in the Top Ten, and in 10 years he may well be No1. Seve should be up there, too, but in a Top Ten you can only have ten (and even then I've picked eleven!).

I tell you what, I wish I could pick my Ryder Cup line-up from the players in this book. No disrespect to today's European players, but that really would be one hell of a team!

Sam Torrance

Opposite: The Great Triumvirate, from left – JH Taylor, James Braid, Harry Vardon

• Sam's Top 10 •

1= Ben Hogan
   Jack Nicklaus
3 Sam Snead
4 Bobby Jones
5 Lee Trevino
6 Arnold Palmer
7 Tom Watson
8 Sir Henry Cotton
9 Gene Sarazen
10= Nick Faldo
    Gary Player

Ben Hogan: 1953 Open winner

Introduction

by Peter Cossins

Encyclopedia of Golf
(By Derek Lawrenson, published by Carlton)

1 Jack Nicklaus

2 Ben Hogan

3 Bobby Jones

4 Arnold Palmer

5 Gary Player

6 Tom Watson

7 Sam Snead

8 Walter Hagen

9 Seve Ballesteros

9a Tiger Woods

10 Gene Sarazen

Tiger Woods: A future all-time great

Arranging great players in any sport in ranking order is always going to be an impossible task, and golf is no different. After much scribbling and crossing out, I opted for a method based on Major tournaments won, other tournaments won and time at the top of the various orders of merit and rankings tables.

However, it soon became clear that this method was going to be only partly satisfactory as it ranked some very good players such as Larry Nelson above some truly great players, notably Tiger Woods.

Add to this the fact that golf's pioneers for a long time had only one Major to compete for and the comparative advantage American players have in tackling three on home soil, and it was clear the method was less than watertight, particularly when the great women players were taken into account.

Ultimately my method became one of tournaments won added to impact on the game, and I also took into account the breadth of competition that now exists in the game compared to even 40 or 50 years ago. The list leans towards American players because for so long they have proved themselves to be the ones to beat, and it is only in recent decades that a host of players from Europe, South Africa and Australia have consistently threatened US domination of

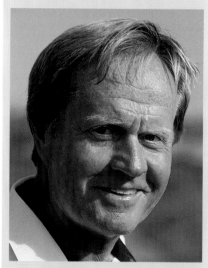

Jack Nicklaus: Everybody's No 1

the sport. In his excellent *Encyclopedia of Golf* (Carlton), Derek Lawrenson circumvents the problem of Woods having only two Majors to his credit by giving him a 9a rating alongside Seve Ballesteros, but it now seems just a matter of time before the young American phenomenon is challenging for a place among golf's widely-agreed top three of Nicklaus, Hogan and Jones.

A poll of fans on the PGA Tour and GolfWeb internet sites at the end of 1999 provided a far different top 10 that featured only one non-American – Greg Norman – and two players who have been the most popular of recent years, the late and sadly

PGA Tour Fans' Poll

1 Jack Nicklaus
2 Tiger Woods
3 Arnold Palmer
4 Ben Hogan
5 Bobby Jones
6 Payne Stewart
7 Fred Couples
8 Byron Nelson
9 Greg Norman
10 Sam Snead

Payne Stewart: Favourite with many fans

Arnold Palmer: General of the Army

missed Payne Stewart and former Masters champion Fred Couples, while Spanish teenager Sergio Garcia's 12th place underlines the impact 'El Niño' has had on the sport in such a short time.

A similar poll among European fans would no doubt turn up a vastly different result, surely featuring Ballesteros, Tony Jacklin and Nick Faldo.

A final comparison is offered by the record book itself. Conveniently, 10 (male) players stand clear of the rest with seven or more Majors to their credit. Of course, there are names missing and there is no one on the list who has won a Major since 1986, but it is hard to make a case for any of these greats being eased too far away from any top 10.

The Record Book

1 Jack Nicklaus 18 Majors
2 Walter Hagen 11
3= Ben Hogan 9
Gary Player 9
5 Tom Watson 8
6= Harry Vardon 7
Bobby Jones 7
Gene Sarazen 7
Sam Snead 7
Arnold Palmer 7

WILLS'S CIGARETTES.

WALTER J. HAGEN.

Walter Hagen: A major Major winner

Jack Nicklaus

'I don't think you would have missed it, but I did not want to give you the chance.'
Nicklaus to Tony Jacklin after giving him the 3ft putt
that meant the 1969 Ryder Cup was tied

O n record alone 'The Golden Bear' stands a golden head and shoulders clear of the rest but, though singularly driven to succeed, Nicklaus has never forgotten the principles of sportsmanship that underpin the game. His 18 Major titles put him a street ahead of the rest, but he has also finished second or third another 28 times and has always been the first to acknowledge the better man on the day.

Nicklaus burst on to a scene dominated by Arnold Palmer and – as a chubby 22-year-old with two US Amateur titles to his credit – immediately snatched the 1962 US Open from under Arnie's nose in a play-off at the Oakmont club that was right in Palmer's back yard. It was a statement of how things were going to be. Nicklaus might have been the bad guy as far as Arnie's Army were concerned, but as Palmer's star waned, Big Jack just kept on winning.

Hugely powerful off the tee, accurate with his irons and a tremendous putter, there were no fundamental weaknesses in his game, which helps to explain why he was so consistently good for so

Nicklaus stunned the game with his 1986 Masters win, left and opposite, 23 years after he first won the title – and 20 years after his first triumph in The Open at Muirfield, right

Nicklaus *factfile*

Born: 21.1.1940, Columbus, Ohio
Country: USA
Major victories: 18 (British Open 1966, 1970, 1978, US Open 1962, 1967, 1972, 1980, US Masters 1963, 1965, 1966, 1972, 1975, 1986, US PGA 1963, 1971, 1973, 1975, 1980)

long. Add his ceaseless desire for titles and you have to wonder how he managed to find the energy to devote so much time to his five children and his golf course design business, Golden Bear Inc. Nicklaus's career at the top lasted longer than anyone's, but only because he twice came back when many had prematurely written him off, most notably when he charged past Greg Norman and Seve Ballesteros, then the top two players in the world, to win the 1986 Masters. Looking back at Big Jack's career, it is perhaps best to recall Bobby Jones's words after Nicklaus had won the 1963 Masters: 'He plays a game with which I am not familiar.'

Ben Hogan

'Shoot a lower score than everyone else.'
Hogan's reply when Nick Faldo asked him what was
the secret to winning the US Open

Hogan's life and career was filled with huge tragedy and unprecedented success. After his father had committed suicide when Hogan was just nine, young Ben took on all the odd jobs he could to supplement the family income, including caddying. From this difficult background came both his love of golf and steely desire to reach the top.

Although initially successful when he became a pro in the 1930s, Hogan focused on perfecting his game, grooving his swing for hour after hour on the practice range and turning up for tournaments several days early in order to get fully acquainted with every aspect of a course. Intense concentration on the job in hand meant that the apparently cold and aloof Texan, nicknamed 'The Iceman', was for a long time respected rather than loved by the galleries.

Deprived by the Second World War of what seemed likely to be his best years, Hogan quickly made up for lost time by winning his first Major in 1946, but early in 1949 he was seriously injured in a car crash. For some months it seemed he would never walk again, let alone return to golf, but that icy will carried him through and a year later he was back to his brilliant best. Though he was constantly troubled by pain in his legs and never again played in the US PGA, which demanded two rounds in a day,

in 1953 Hogan pulled off the still unmatched feat of winning three Majors in a single season, and after returning home victorious from his only visit to the British Open he received a ticker-tape welcome in New York.

Virtually unbeatable at that time, Hogan had won eight of his last 11 Majors.

Hogan *factfile*

Born: 13.8.1912, Dublin, Texas
Died: 1997
Country: USA
Major victories: 9 (British Open 1953, US Open 1948, 1950, 1951, 1953, US Masters 1951, 1953, US PGA 1946, 1948)

Ben Hogan, left with the 'baseball-style' putting grip he adopted during his career, walked away with the only British Open he entered, in 1953 (above)

Keeping up with the Joneses: The American sealed his second successive British Open in 1927, above, and went on to dominate golf for three years before retiring early

Bobby Jones

Jones *factfile*

Born: 17.3.1902, Atlanta, Georgia
Died: 1971
Country: USA
Major victories: 7 (British Open 1926, 1927, 1930, US Open 1923, 1926, 1929, 1930)

Not happy with winning seven Majors, Jones created another, the Masters at Augusta

3

Surprisingly, the greatest amateur golfer of all time was nervous on the course, chain-smoked, shied away from the crowds and even lost weight because he had trouble eating. But no one has achieved as much as Bobby Jones did in his short golfing career: six amateur titles, seven Majors and a 'grand slam' in 1930 ... and golf was not even his main interest.

Blessed with a smooth and powerful swing, Jones never gave up his amateur status and regarded the game almost as a secondary career. For nine months of the year he immersed himself in studying for the Bar, the other three he gave over to golf, making what he

'I could take out of my life everything except my experiences at St Andrews and I'd still have a rich, full life.'

achieved even more remarkable. He was a prodigious talent from an early age but was initially held back by a fearsome temper. Only when he conquered his anger did the Major titles flow.

A slight figure, Jones was meticulous in his tournament preparation and from 1923 won 13 British and US Amateur and Open championships. His 'grand slam' of the Amateur and Open titles on both sides of the Atlantic is an achievement that will probably never be repeated. Having retired from competitive golf at just 28 and set up a law firm in Atlanta, he established the only Major that is always played on the same course, the Masters.

Jones bought the land, developed the course and in 1934 hosted his first invitational tournament. The course and tournament now stand as a memorial to the greatest amateur of all.

Arnold Palmer

Golf can be divided into two eras: Before Palmer and After Palmer. Before 'Arnie' exploded on to the scene in the mid-'50s, golf was a minority sport that attracted little media or corporate attention. Within a few years it had been transformed as Palmer's aggressive playing approach and charisma took the game to the masses and brought huge television attention and the interest of big business.

The son of a club professional, Palmer had a simple philosophy: 'If you can see it, you can hole it.' Booming huge drives off the tee, attacking with his irons and not afraid to knock a putt three feet past if it gave him a chance to hole it, Palmer quickly pulled in large and boisterous galleries, dubbed 'Arnie's Army', who liked nothing better than to see him reduce a course and the competition to their knees. Not only did he pull golf

Arnold Palmer changed the face of golf, winning dozens of trophies such as the 1967 World Matchplay, above – but, more importantly, he dragged the game into the television age with the help of the famous Arnie's Army

Palmer *factfile*

Born: 10.9.1929, Latrobe, Pennsylvania
Country: USA
Major victories: 7 (British Open 1961, 1962, US Open 1960, US Masters 1958, 1960, 1962, 1964)

'What other people may find in poetry or art, I find in the flight of a good drive.'

into the television age but he can also be credited with saving the British Open. Overlooked by the top Americans in the 50s, Palmer loved the links game at first sight and encouraged his colleagues to make the annual trip across the Atlantic. Though, amazingly, he won no Majors after 1964 and was soon eclipsed by Jack Nicklaus, for many years he remained the top earner and even now is one of the world's most popular sportsmen.

For, despite all the wealth, private jets and adulation, Arnie has remained a man of the people, chatting with the galleries and providing support to worthy causes, from offering sports scholarships to building children's hospitals. Not the best player of all time, but certainly the one who has been the most loved and made the greatest impact.

Hagen *factfile*

Born: 21.12.1892, Rochester, New York
Died: 1969, Traverse City, Michigan
Country: USA
Major victories: 11
(US Open 1914, 1919,
British Open 1922, 1924, 1928,
1929, US PGA 1921, 1924, 1925,
1926, 1927)

Walter Hagen

Much like Arnold Palmer in the 1960s and Tiger Woods in the 1990s, the dapper and larger-than-life Walter Hagen created huge public interest in golf and was fundamental in modernising the game in the 1920s, becoming the sport's first millionaire in the process. Always immaculately turned out in a silk shirt and perfectly pressed plus twos, Hagen had a reputation as a high roller and a

'In life always take time to smell the flowers along the way.'
Hagen's favourite saying

womaniser, and always travelled the circuit with a black book filled with, as he put it, 'the names of friendly natives'. But on the course

his reputation was as a supremely confident tactician who had the ability to extricate himself from the most horrendous of lies with almost arrogant ease. His first Major success came in the US Open in 1914, a victory he repeated in 1919, but it was in the British Open and the US PGA that Hagen cemented

18

his image of flamboyance and unwavering skill and determination. Hagen first went to the British Open in 1922 and arrived at Sandwich in a chauffeur-driven limousine.

As a professional in a still very stuffy amateur-dominated sport, Hagen found that he was not allowed to enter the clubhouse and changed on the back seat. He went on to win the championship, becoming the first American-born golfer to do so. Hagen picked up another three Open titles but surpassed even this total in the US PGA, which he won five times in seven seasons. Then arranged under a matchplay format, the US PGA always

Hagen, opposite, hands over the Ryder Cup on his arrival in Britain in 1929. He captained the US team to four victories in the famous match, attracting the attention of the Prince of Wales, above, in 1933

revealed Hagen at his confident best, chatting to the adoring gallery between shots and overwhelming opponents with a mixture of consistent and outrageous play.

The dominant golfer of the mid-1920s, Hagen's matchplay talent led to his appointment as captain of the US team for the first Ryder Cup tournament in 1927. Under his leadership the Americans trounced the Great

Britain and Ireland team 9½-2½ at Worcester, Massachusetts.

Despite his 11 Majors, it is the legend of Hagen the showman that persists. He not only made a million from golf, but spent it all.

Never one for a good night's rest before a big tournament, more than once Hagen arrived on the first tee still in his dinner suit having been out all night. However, despite living the high life, to this day Hagen's record in Major tournaments has only been eclipsed by Jack Nicklaus, and for many the American remains the greatest exponent of the recovery shot the game has ever seen.

Gary Player

'I am a great believer that age is only a number.'

Dubbed the 'Black Knight' for the monochrome attire that became his trademark, the combative South African formed, together with Arnold Palmer and Jack Nicklaus, the triumvirate who dominated the sport in the 1960s.

In fact, the celebrated broadcaster and journalist Henry Longhurst believed the diminutive Player was the best golfer of all time for the simple fact that, unlike the other pretenders to that title, he won all of his Majors on foreign soil, making his haul of nine titles doubly

Player *factfile*

Born: 1.11.1935, Johannesburg
Country: South Africa
Major victories: 9 (British Open 1959, 1968, 1974,
US Open 1965, US Masters 1961, 1974, 1978,
US PGA 1962, 1972)

Player is still going strong, and still wearing black, more than 40 years after his first Major win, opposite

impressive. The son of a gold miner, he has spent his entire career showing people that they were wrong to say his swing was too unorthodox to get him anywhere, his frame too small to compete with the game's big hitters, that he was washed up before he won his final Major at the age of 42. His swing is not a thing of beauty, but obsessive practice and questioning of his peers made it consistent, and once near the greens there have been few golfers more deadly, especially from bunkers.

Also obsessive about staying in shape, and even now a force on the Seniors Tour, Player follows an intense training regime and is said to be strong enough to do 100 press-ups with a suitcase full of clothes on his back. The combination of practice, fitness and focus enabled him to stay at the top for more than two decades and made him the third man, after Gene Sarazen and Ben Hogan, to win all four Majors.

Tiger Woods

'Tiger Woods is the most important thing that has happened in golf for 50 years.'
Tom Watson

Woods is quite simply a phenomenon. He has redefined golf, ushering in multi-million-pound endorsements and opening the game up to an audience well beyond the usual white, male middle-class followers. Son of an African-American father and a Thai mother and named after one of his father's army friends in Vietnam, he was playing golf literally almost as soon as he could walk, and as an amateur rewrote pretty much every record in the book.

He turned pro in 1996 and won two of the season's remaining seven events. If that was breathtaking, what followed was unheard of as he swept into his first Major, the Masters, and waltzed off with the Green Jacket by a record 12 shots. Viewing figures went through the roof, as did sales of Nike golf equipment.

His long, sweeping swing generates huge power, often leaving him a short iron to the green on even long par fives. But, as with all true greats, he has the touch, course management and putting to rub in that advantage. Favourite for every event he enters, Woods hit another level in 1999, winning nine tournaments after sacrificing some of his power for greater control. His streak continued into the new millennium as he equalled Ben Hogan's 1948 record of six successive US Tour victories.

A weakness? Coping with national expectation at the Ryder Cup, where he has lost six games in 10, seems the only chink in his armour. Woods has it all and wants more. His father reckons he'll win 14 Majors. As usual with Tiger it seems likely he will live up to the hype.

Woods *factfile*

Born: 30.12.1975, Cypress, California
Country: USA
Major victories: 2
(US Masters 1997, US PGA 1999)

Those Tiger feats: Woods has blown away his rivals in events across the world, from the '97 Masters, opposite, to the '99 World Championships at Valderrama, above

Tom Watson

'The person I fear most in the last two rounds is myself.'

L abelled a 'choker' during the early part of his career, psychology graduate Watson decided after some advice from Byron Nelson that his was not a case of losing but of not knowing how to win. Once the wins did start to come, even Jack Nicklaus could not compete with Watson, who became probably the best links golfer of the post-War era with a succession of spectacular Major victories.

Majestic and supremely accurate from tee to green, at the height of his powers the hole seemed to be as big as a bucket. Putts were holed from all over and if they were missed, usually because he was too bold, he would ram in the return with barely a thought. Five times leading US money winner, Watson fought two great duels with Nicklaus and came out on top both times. Their form was so imperious at the '77 British Open that they finished 11 shots clear.

Never as popular as Nicklaus with the galleries for much the same reasons as when Nicklaus threatened Arnold Palmer's domination, Watson's mental strength gradually eroded and the bad old days returned on the greens. Often in contention, he couldn't make the five-footers when he had to. For a time he turned to drink, but showed his character with a popular US Tour win in 1997 at the age of 48.

Watson *factfile*

Born: 4.9.1949, Kansas City, Missouri
Country: USA
Major victories: 8
(British Open 1975, 1977, 1980, 1982, 1983, US Open 1982, US Masters 1977, 1981)

Watson was often his own worst enemy, especially on the greens, but his superb links play ensured an amazing dominance in his beloved British Open, left

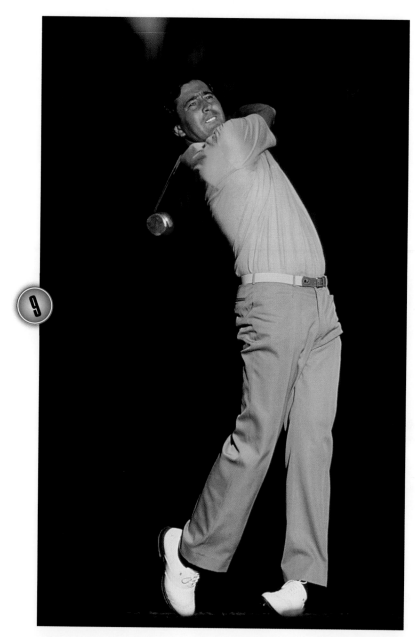

9

Severiano Ballesteros

*A*rguably the most natural talent the sport has ever seen, the handsome, passionate and always demonstrative Spaniard almost single-handedly revitalised the game in Europe. The youngest of three golfing brothers, Ballesteros's first experience of golf was as a caddie, and his first club a three iron with which he practised on the local beach. Using this one club the young Seve

'Seve's got shots the rest of us don't even know.'
Ben Crenshaw

The Sun King: Ballesteros went from playing on a Spanish beach to wowing the crowds as a multiple Major winner and becoming the scourge of the Americans in the Ryder Cup

Ballesteros *factfile*

Born: 9.4.1957, Pedrena
Country: Spain
Major victories: 5 (British Open 1979, 1984, 1988, US Masters 1980, 1983)

The famous Seve celebration, fist clenched, arms pumping, head shaking, witnessed above after holing a putt on the 18th to win the 1984 Open at St Andrews, was a common sight across the world in the 1980s as the charismatic Spaniard fashioned some amazing victories

was able to fashion absolutely any shot he wanted, and this experience became the basis for a magical short game that more often than not got him out of the trouble his wayward driving had put him into.

Dubbed the 'car park champion' by the US press after he played a shot from in one at the 1979 Open and often annoyingly introduced as 'Steve' to American galleries, the highly charged Spaniard provided the perfect riposte by beating every-one out of sight at the 1980 Masters, becoming the first European to wear the Green Jacket. Fiercely proud of his roots and never happier

'I've never seen somebody miss so many fairways and win.'
Hale Irwin after the 1979 British Open

than when putting the Americans in their place, Seve was instrumental in reviving the fortunes of the Ryder Cup as the format was expanded to allow Europeans to compete. Once Ballesteros had showed his colleagues they could take on the best, European golf advanced to new heights.

Hampered by constant back pain that made it difficult to play consistently at a high level in the 1990s, Ballesteros is still a great favourite with fans: glowering, committed and still likely to conjure up some magic from a part of the course no one else has visited.

Nick Faldo

'I have never met a more focused professional.'
Faldo's former coach David Leadbetter

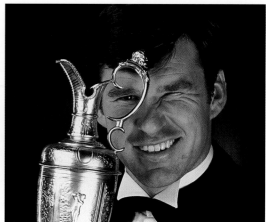

I nspired to take up golf when he watched on the TV as Jack Nicklaus won the 1972 US Masters, Faldo has gone from being the youngest ever British amateur champion and a prolific winner on the European Tour, to almost certainly the best British golfer of all time. While he boasts natural talent aplenty, the Englishman's rise can be put down to his complete dedication to his game and a relentless drive to achieve success on the biggest stages, a drive which often left a clear divide between his fans and critics.

To achieve this rise, Faldo had his swing taken apart by one of a new breed of coaching gurus, David Leadbetter. From being No 1 on the European Tour in 1983 his standing crumbled as student and teacher worked together to iron out the kinks that were prevent-

Faldo *factfile*

Born: 18.7.57, Welwyn Garden City
Country: England
Major victories: 6
(British Open 1987, 1990, 1992,
US Masters 1989, 1990, 1996)

**Blooming gorgeous: Faldo fell in love
with the azalea-strewn Masters and
has won in Augusta three times, but
he is essentially a very British
champion – his Masters meal in 1997
was a supper of fish and chips**

ing Faldo making his great leap forward. Few golfers would have put up with four years in the wilderness but when Faldo's new swing was put to the ultimate test at the 1987 British Open it stood up to the pressure as those around him wilted.

Though functional rather than elegant, there is no denying the effectiveness of Faldo's revamped swing and by the late 1980s he was everyone's favourite for every Major. Accurate driving and iron play regularly put him in contention at the tight courses set up for the US Open and US PGA, and a perfectly honed putting stroke enabled him to emulate his hero Nicklaus by winning back-to-back Masters titles.

It remains to be seen whether Faldo can emulate Harry Vardon's total of seven Majors, the best by a Briton. He has not won a Major since sacking Leadbetter and was 'sacked' by his caddie at the end of 1999. But he has been written off before.

Sam Snead

Hailing from the backwoods of Virginia, where his first 'clubs' were fashioned from the limbs of a swamp maple tree, 'Slammin' Sam' is one of golf's great natural talents. A budding American football star, Snead switched sports when he sustained a back injury and immediately mastered all aspects of his new career, particularly the booming drives that gave him his nickname.

Snead was a remarkable golfer in many ways: he still holds the record for wins on the US Tour with 81; he was the first man to shoot 59 in competition; and he was the first pro to score below his age

11

when he shot 67, 66 in the Quad Cities Open at the age of 67. A winner in six different decades, Snead's record stands comparison with the sport's greats, but a tendency towards impulsiveness often got the better of a talent so sublime that he never felt the need to spend long periods practising. In the 1950s it was said that if Snead's beautifully smooth swing and all-round brilliance

> *'If I had shot 69 in the last round I would have won nine US Opens'*
> Snead, probably the best player never to win that title

could be placed under Ben Hogan's head the resulting golfer would be close to invincible.

Snead's only British Open success came at St Andrews after he had been loudly and typically critical of a course he compared to a 'cow pasture'. He was equalling scathing about the surrounding facilities and local food. Yet, despite occasional outbursts, Snead was and remains a favourite of the galleries, who still flock to see him as one of the honorary starters at the Masters.

Snead *factfile*

Born: 27.5.1912, Ashwood, Virginia
Country: USA
Major victories: 7 (British Open 1946, US Masters 1949, 1952, 1954, USPGA 1942, 1949, 1951)

Slammin' Sam shows Carnoustie a glimpse of his talent in 1937

Every time a golfer steps into a greenside bunker they should give thanks to Sarazen, who developed the wide-soled club now known as the sand wedge. Born Eugenio Saraceni into very humble beginnings, Sarazen seemed likely to follow his father into the family carpentry business, but when working as a teenage apprentice in the wood shop he was taken ill and told to work outdoors

Gene Sarazen

Playing with Fred Daly and Max Faulkner in the 1973 British Open at Troon, Sarazen holed-in-one at the famous 'Postage Stamp' par-three eighth hole. The next day he holed out from a bunker for a two. He was 71.

12

Gentleman Gene at the 1928 Open at Sandwich, left, and above in 1994

Sarazen factfile

Born: 27.2.1902, Harrison, New York
Died: 1999
Country: USA
Major victories: 7 (British Open 1932, US Open 1922, 1932, US Masters 1935, US PGA 1922, 1923, 1933)

away from the dust. Already a keen golfer, Sarazen took a job as assistant at a local club and a rags-to-riches story was under way.

Sarazen's career is one of firsts: the first man to win two Majors in a season (1922), the first professional to win the British and US Opens in the same season (1932), and the first man to win all four Majors in his career. Given Sarazen's poverty-stricken background it is understandable that at the height of his powers in the 1930s he toured the globe playing in lucrative challenge matches rather than focusing on tournaments, though in the process he did become the highest-paid sportsman in the world.

Sarazen is best remembered as the man who hit the shot that put the Masters on the map. Three down with four to play, Sarazen holed his second at the par-five 15th, tied Craig Wood and won the play-off. Proud and courageous, he continued to shoot good scores into his 70s and acted as honorary starter at the Masters until 1998 when he was 96.

Vardon *factfile*

Born: 9.5.1870, Grouville, Jersey
Died: 1937
Major victories: 7 (British Open 1896, 1898, 1899, 1903, 1911, 1914, US Open 1900)

Harry Vardon

A regular visitor to the US, Vardon avoided likely death when injury forced him out of a transatlantic trip on the Titanic in 1912

The most prolific British Major winner, Vardon, left in 1934, has given his name to the European money winner trophy

The only man ever to win the British Open six times, Channel Islander Vardon was a golfing contradiction, playing with great style and accuracy from tee to green, but suffering so severely with the yips that Gene Sarazen described him as 'the most atrocious putter I have ever seen'.

Best remembered as the originator of the overlapping grip still taught today, he in fact popularised a technique first used by British amateur champion Johnny Laidlaw. Vardon followed his brother Tom to England and into golf, and after some minor success was made pro at Ganton Golf Club in Yorkshire. The members there were so impressed with Vardon's ability that they raised enough money to host a challenge match with British Open champion JH Taylor, which Vardon won comprehensively. A few weeks later he succeeded Taylor as Open champion.

Together with James Braid, these two golfers dominated the sport before the First World War, but Vardon was the only one of the Great Triumvirate to claim a US Open title. Struck down by tuberculosis in 1903, Vardon was never quite the same player again, although he was runner-up at the US Open as late as 1920.

Lee Trevino

'Pressure is playing for five bucks when you've got two bucks in your pocket.'

Treesy does it: Trevino on his way to a comeback victory in the 1984 US PGA

Trevino *factfile*

Born: 1.12.1939, Dallas, Texas
Country: USA
Major victories: 6 (British Open 1971, 1972, US Open 1968, 1971, US PGA 1974, 1984)

14

The illegitimate son of a Mexican grave-digger who was brought up in a shack without electricity and running water and first ventured on to a golf course to look for lost balls he could sell, 'Supermex' has risen from the most humble of beginnings to become one of the most successful and popular players of recent decades.

With a home-made swing so ungainly it looked like he would topple over and a hooker's grip, Trevino first astounded the golf world and then, against everyone's predictions, kept astounding them. Though his peers often wondered how he kept the ball in play, the Mexican-American was supremely skilled at working it in whichever direction was needed and for a time at the start of the 1970s was so inspirational on and around the greens that he topped the US money list and scooped a handful of Majors. Trevino's playing origins were as a hustler moving from one Texan course to the next taking whatever bets he could get, and often betting more than he had. The streetwise image was completed by a constant stream of banter, usually poking fun at himself, that eventually made him a crowd favourite. Bizarrely, away from the course he has always been private and somewhat of a loner.

When at his peak, Trevino was struck by lightning and suffered back injuries so severe he could barely practise. It seemed his career was over, but, once again showing his innate tenacity, he fought back to claim a US PGA title with four rounds below 70 and later went on to dominate the US Seniors Tour, where he is still a wise-cracking favourite.

Opinions are divided on Nelson's status among the leading golfers because many of his greatest victories coincided with a time when many of his potential rivals were still in the armed forces. However, so phenomenal were the Texan's achievements during this period that it is fair to assume he was in a zone no one else could have reached.

Remarkably, Nelson's first links with golf were made as a caddie at the same club as Ben Hogan and their careers ran in tandem, though Nelson was the first to snag a Major. He took three more by the time golf came to a halt for the war, in which Nelson was

15

Nelson's 11 tournament-winning run in 1945 went from March 11 to August 4. His stroke average for the season was 68.33.

Byron Nelson

Nelson *factfile*

Born: 4.2.1912, Fort Worth, Texas
Country: USA
Major victories: 5
(US Open 1939, US Masters 1937, 1942, US PGA 1940, 1945)

Before a surprisingly early retirement to a ranch in Texas, Byron Nelson set a series of extraordinary records in 1945 that will probably never be equalled

exempted from service because of his haemophilia. When competition began again in 1945 Nelson was nigh on unbeatable. One of the first to play with steel-shafted clubs, which provided more consistency and greater distance, he used neither the draw nor fade favoured by his contemporaries, opting instead for straight hitting.

Though the competition could have been harder, Nelson won 18 of the 30 tournaments he played in that year, a record 11 of them in a row, averaging fewer than 68 shots a round in the process. When he retired from competitive golf in 1946 to live on the ranch in Texas he had been saving his winnings to buy, Nelson had played in 113 tournaments in the 1940s and finished in the top 10 in all of them. Later he acted as mentor to Tom Watson, advising his protégé that if he played to his potential the Major victories would come, and hosted the tournament that carries his name.

Greg Norman

In 1986 Norman led all of the four Majors going into the last round but won only one, the British Open

*T*he 'Great White Shark' holds an unenviable place in golf's annals as the only man to have lost a play-off at all four Majors, and his record of just two Major wins does huge disservice to his ability and longevity at the top of the game.

With his blond hair flowing alongside a fast and powerful swing, Norman has long been one of the most popular and charismatic golfers, drawing large galleries whether he is challenging for the lead or making up the numbers. Indeed, part of his attraction, particularly at the Majors, is that something breathtaking is always likely to happen. He may produce spell-binding golf, linking massive and accurate hitting with pinpoint irons and superb touch, and blow everyone away, or – and this, unfortunately, has been more likely – he may establish a commanding lead only to snatch defeat from the jaws of victory.

The long-time world No 1 has been on the receiving end of more than his fair share of outrageous bad luck. Bob Tway at the 1986 US PGA and Larry Mize at the 1987 Masters both holed from off the green to deny Norman cruelly for their only Major wins. But he has also brought disaster on himself, choking spectacularly in all of the American Majors, notably in the 1996 Masters when he lost to Nick Faldo after holding a six-shot last-round lead.

Norman now oversees a huge worldwide business empire, but even at 45, recovering from a major shoulder injury and with all the private jets he needs, the Australian is keen to secure his place in history.

16

The Shark bites: The flamboyant Norman has won only two Majors, both British Opens

Norman *factfile*

Born: 10.2.1955, Queensland
Country: Australia
Major victories: 2
(British Open 1986, 1993)

Young Tom Morris

'Deeply regretted by numerous friends and all golfers, he thrice in succession won the Championship Belt and held it without envy, his many amiable qualities being no less acknowledged than his golfing achievements.'

Inscription on Young Tom's gravestone

Son of 'Old Tom', this all-conquering Scot was the first player to dominate the British Open, winning four in a row and forcing the organising committee to come up with a new format for the tournament. But perhaps it's no surprise, for the Open was then held every year at Prestwick, where his illustrious father had been greenkeeper and pro.

17

When Morris completed a hat-trick of wins and claimed the championship belt as his own, the organisers took a year off to decide how to develop the tournament. They came back with an event that rotated between three venues and offered the famous Claret Jug as its trophy. Young Tom came back and won the title for the fourth time in a row, once again at Prestwick.

Unfortunately, as he came off the course at North Berwick after a challenge match in 1875, Morris was given the news that his wife had been taken seriously ill during childbirth and she died before he could get home. Stricken with grief, just a few months later Young Tom also passed away. He was just 24.

Morris *factfile*

Born: 20.4.1851, St Andrews
Died: 25.12.1875
Country: Scotland
Major victories: 4 (British Open 1868, 1869, 1870, 1872)

Young Tom wearing the British Open Championship belt he won three times in a row

Wright *factfile*

Born: 14.2.1935,
San Diego, California
Country: USA
Major victories: 13 (US Open
1958, 1959, 1961, 1964,
US LPGA 1958, 1960, 1961,
1963, Titleholders Championship
1961, 1962, Western Open 1962,
1963, 1966)

Mickey taker: Wright dominated the
US Open, above, in the 1960s

Mickey Wright

*'A good golf swing has always been more
important to me than scoring well.'*

Arguably the best natural talent the women's game has ever seen, Mary Kathryn 'Mickey' Wright came into the game from the same University of Stanford golf programme that later produced Tom Watson and Tiger Woods and she enjoyed the same kind of dominance over the women's game that those two greats did over the men's. Not only did she possess the nearest thing to a perfect swing the women's game has seen, but she had an armoury of shots which could get her out of almost any trouble. Wright's dominance coincided with Arnold Palmer's, which may explain why her exploits are sometimes overlooked.

At the turn of the 1960s the gap between her and the opposition was so marked she was expected to win, and, at an average of one in every four tournaments, she did. In 1961 she won three of the four events that then made up the grand slam, and two years later set a record of 13 wins from 32 starts. A reticent figure who shied away from the spotlight, she effectively retired in 1969 with foot and wrist injuries.

The oldest player (51) in Ryder Cup history, he's lost more matches than any other American simply because he's played more than any other. The only man besides Sam Snead to win a US Tour event in four different decades, Floyd is now a leading force on the US Senior Tour and still fixing rivals with that soul-destroying stare.

The eyes have it: Ray Floyd's success has spanned four different decades, and he is still going strong

Ray Floyd

Floyd *factfile*

In eight seasons on the Senior Tour Floyd has won almost three times as much as he did in 30 on the PGA Tour, and almost $20 million in total

Hardened golfers have crumbled when confronted with it, snap-happy photographers have blanched when the focus of it, and few could ignore what Payne Stewart described as 'the Raymond Floyd stare', a look that would burn through rivals, erode their confidence and leave the burly American to collect the spoils. A natural talent with a brute of a swing that would find no favour with today's golfing gurus, Floyd initially partied harder than he played, at one stage managing an all-girl rock band. However, when he did apply himself to golf wholeheartedly the titles soon came.

A great motivator of others in Ryder Cup matches and of himself in any situation, at his peak he was deadly within pitching distance of the green and was one of the few golfing greats who thrived on pressure, in his case the pressure of leading from a long way out and keeping his pursuers at arm's length. He led both the 1976 Masters and 1982 USPGA from start to finish, in the former charging clear of the pack to win by eight strokes.

Born: 4.9.1942, Fort Bragg, North Carolina
Country: USA
Major victories: 4
(US Open 1986, US Masters 1976, USPGA 1969, 1982)

Thomson *factfile*

Born: 23.8.1929, Melbourne
Country: Australia
Major victories: 5 (British Open 1954, 1955, 1956, 1958, 1965)

Thomson had little time for the 'target golf' courses in America, preferring the test of links play

himself against a course, thinking his way round it and thrived on links courses where a score had to be worked for and earned. He scorned the American focus on target golf and, though he has a fair record in US tournaments, found many of the courses over-dependent on man-made features.

20

Peter Thomson

'The great player has one vital quality: calmness.'

Sometimes under-rated because four of his Open titles were claimed when the top American players had turned their backs on the championship, Australia's first great champion is something of a golfing enigma. The only man this century to win three consecutive British Opens and 'champion golfer' five times in all, he had relatively little success in the United States until he joined the Senior Tour full time in

1985 and then he won nine tournaments and $1 million in a season. Yet almost as soon as he had made an impact in the US, Thomson grew bored with it and returned to his other interests of course design, commentary, journalism and the arts.

Strong with his irons and calm under pressure, he silenced some of the doubters with victory over the likes of Player, Palmer and Nicklaus in 1965. Thomson liked to pit

ing her unwell, but returned for the '29 British event because it was at St Andrews and won it again. Manager of golf at Fortnum & Mason in London, she played exhibitions with the likes of Sir Henry Cotton, who said: 'No golfer has stood out so far ahead of his or her contemporaries.'

Queen of the course: Wethered in 1925

Wethered *factfile*

Born: 17.11.1901, Surrey
Died: 1997
Country: England
Major victories: 0

JOYCE WETHERED

Joyce Wethered

'I have never played against anyone and felt so outclassed.'
Bobby Jones

Reckoned by many, including Bobby Jones, to be the best woman golfer ever and by some to be the best golfer full stop, Wethered's ability was so prodigious that she could have earned a place on the Walker Cup team, and would have been one of the better players. Never a tournament pro, the later Lady Heathcote-Amory played golf as a girl with her brother, Roger, who was to be a professional.

Her swing was smooth and compact, and her timing so precise she outhit her female rivals by a considerable margin and in matches against leading men – from the same tees – was more than capable of holding her own, despite the fact she would have been dwarfed by the likes of Laura Davies. From 1920 to 1924 she was unbeaten at the English Ladies' Open and won the British title three times in four years. She retired in 1925 claiming the pressure was mak-

Sir Henry Cotton

Cotton *factfile*

Born: 26.1.1907, Holmes Chapel
Died: 1987
Country: England
Major victories: 3 (British Open 1934, 1937, 1948)

22

Henry Cotton at St Andrews in 1927

'The best is always
good enough for me.'
Henry Cotton

Dapper and flamboyant, Cotton was the British equivalent of Walter Hagen, a golfer who played exquisitely on the course and lived the high life off it. Son of a rich industrialist, he took up golf at public school when banned from playing cricket for refusing the cane. At 16 he was playing in the British Open and by 20 he was among the contenders for the title.

As Cotton emerged on to the scene, the Americans were dominating the sport and he crossed the Atlantic to find the game was treated more seriously and prize funds were much higher. Cotton returned determined to earn what he believed he was worth and in doing so he pulled the British game into the modern era. A natural talent, his swing complemented his champagne lifestyle and this potent mix boosted the galleries, which in turn boosted the rewards on offer. One of the first British sportsmen to explore the potential of commerical contracts, he is inextricably linked with golf equipment maker Dunlop.

On the way to his first British Open title in 1934, Cotton shot 65 in the second round, which would remain a record until 1977 and was then deemed a feat so extraordinary that Dunlop named its new ball the '65'. But for the Second World War, Cotton would surely have won more titles.

Johnny Miller

'The best thing that ever happened to me was coming second in the 1971 Masters. I couldn't have coped if I'd won.'

When Johnny Miller followed his US Open victory with eight US Tour wins in the 1974 season it seemed the tall, handsome and typically blond Californian was destined to scoop a host of Majors but, much like Curtis Strange in the 1980s, Miller's haul ended at two, a total that did scant justice to his ability.

A streaky putter who could be unbeatable one week and an also-ran the next, Miller, a strict Mormon with six children, focused increasingly on his family and less on his game. A master of long-iron play on his day, the simple fact was that Miller quickly achieved a great deal, ensuring his financial stability, and soon got bored with a routine that kept him away from his family for so much of the year.

Both his Major victories were remarkable because he made two of the world's toughest courses, Oakmont and Royal Birkdale, appear child's play. His closing round of 63 at the 1973 US Open was a long-time record for a final round in a Major and emphasized his strengths – laser-like accuracy to the greens followed by nerveless putting.

Blessed with a long and graceful swing, Miller is now an occasional competitor on the US Senior Tour, but devotes more of his time to course design and TV, where he has become a blunt but always insightful commentator.

Seventies style: Miller claims the British Open in 1976

Miller *factfile*

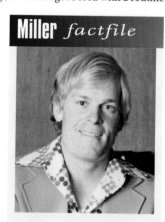

Born: 29.4.1947, San Francisco, California
Country: USA
Major victories: 2 (British Open 1976, US Open 1973)

James Braid

Together with Harry Vardon and JH Taylor, Braid was one of the 'Great Triumvirate' who dominated golf from the turn of the century until the start of the First World War. Though Vardon proved to be the best of the trio, Braid was the first to win the British Open five times, a feat he achieved in just 10 years, all of his victories coming in Scotland.

The Scot was introduced to the game at the links course at Elie, a few miles south of St Andrews, by his cousins when he was a small boy, and over the course of his life rarely passed a day without playing a round, and often two, even when well into his 70s. Trained as a carpenter and joiner, Braid made his own clubs and it was this talent which saw him move south, first to work as clubmaker at the Army and Navy Stores in London and later as the long-serving club pro at Walton Heath, where he played a major part in developing their two courses.

A big hitter both off the tee and with his irons, the modest and dignified Braid was skilled around the green but often struggled with his putting. A change from a wooden-headed to a metal-headed putter helped correct this relative weakness and put him on the path to Open success. A founder member of the PGA, Braid's farming background in Fife was instrumental in his success as a course designer, which led to work on 200 courses, including Carnoustie and Gleneagles.

Braid *factfile*

Born: 6.2.1870, Earlsferry
Died: 1950
Country: Scotland
Major victories: 5 (British Open 1901, 1905, 1906, 1908, 1910)

Braid was a hugely influential figure in golf's development in Britain, not just as a supreme player with five Open wins

'This tall, stooping, ruddy complexioned Scot is one of the wonders of the golfing world.'
Sir Henry Cotton on James Braid

Taylor *factfile*

Born: 19.3.1871, Northiam
Died: 1963
Country: England
Major victories: 5 (British Open 1894, 1895, 1900, 1909, 1913)

John Henry Taylor

The first member of the 'Great Triumvirate' to rise to prominence at the turn of the 20th century, Taylor, known as 'JH', won the first Open Championship ever to be staged outside Scotland when the tournament was held at Royal St George's in 1894. A stocky and strong man with a personality to match, Taylor thrived when the weather conditions worsened, perhaps as a result of his upbringing on the windy north Devon coast.

In common with all professionals of his era, Taylor's bread and butter was working as a club professional, in his case at Royal Mid-Surrey, where he held the position for 47 years. With James Braid, he was also instrumental in forming the Professional Golfers' Association. Such was his love for competition that Taylor was still competing in the Open at the age of 53 and continued to advise on course design until very late in his life.

Taylor made: JH, left, in 1908, a year before his fourth British Open title, and above in 1901

Nancy Lopez

'Lopez had more pure charisma than any player since the Babe [Zaharias], and the game to go with it.'
Rhonda Glenn, Illustrated History of Women's Golf

In much the same way that Arnold Palmer boosted the men's game in the 1950s, Lopez, with her Latin good looks, beaming smile and all-or-nothing style, lifted the women's game to a new level 20 years later. Her swing may make purists shudder, but she has never held anything back on the tee and has a short game to die for.

Like a marketing man's dream, Lopez came from nowhere in her first season as a pro and carried all before her. Not only was she rookie of the year, she won nine tournaments – five of them in a row – and topped the money list. Extrovert and attractive, she introduced thousands of new disciples to the women's game, and an ability to remain cool under pressure ensured that her initial winning burst continued for several years.

Married to former baseball star Ray Knight, Lopez did briefly lose her momentum when she had her first child in 1983 but, urged on by her husband, who did not want to see her talent go to waste, she returned to top the money list in 1985. Still a force to be reckoned with, her remaining ambition is to win the US Open title that has eluded her. In 1997 she became the first woman to break 70 in every round of the tournament, but was still denied by Britain's Alison Nicholas.

Lopez stunned the women's game with her arrival as a pro in the 1970s and has gone on to ensure herself a major place in the game's history

Lopez *factfile*

Born: 6.1.1957, Torrance, California
Country: USA
Major victories: 3 (US LPGA 1978, 1985, 1989)

Tall, powerful and icy cool under pressure, the 30-year-old South African has all the attributes needed to fulfil his ambition of completing a grand slam of the Majors. Blessed with a wonderfully smooth swing that lets him rip

In 1993 Els became the first man ever to shoot four rounds under 70 in the British Open, but by the end he was only tied for sixth

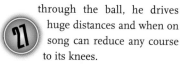

through the ball, he drives huge distances and when on song can reduce any course to its knees.

The first man since his compatriot Gary Player to complete a sweep of the South African Open, PGA and Masters, Els was almost unknown when he joined the US Tour for the first time in 1994 and held his nerve longest to win an 18-hole play-off for the US Open that continued to the 20th hole.

His control and good golf brain make him a threat at any tournament, and particularly at the Masters, where his tendency to fade the ball off the tee works in his favour.

He has also proved a formidable match-play opponent, winning three consecutive World Match Play titles at Wentworth and anchoring South Africa to World Cup and Dunhill Cup triumphs. One of the most outwardly relaxed players in the game – he is

Ernie Els

known as the Big Easy and a smile is never far away – the only potential flaw in his game is a susceptibility to back problems, though occasional spasms have not yet forced him to miss any of the Majors he prizes so dearly.

With age and experience on his side, Els has what it takes to add to his haul and become an all-time great.

Els, named the Big Easy for his huge size and unflappable temperament, is making a big name for himself in Europe and the US

Els *factfile*

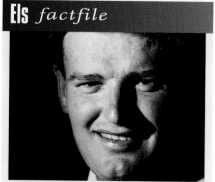

Born: 17.10.1969, Johannesburg
Country: South Africa
Major victories: 2 (US Open 1994, 1997)

Billy Casper

A bear of a man who undeservedly drew more comments for his size than his immense golfing talent, Casper would undoubtedly have won many more Major titles if his time at the top of the golfing tree hadn't coincided with the likes of Jack Nicklaus, Arnold Palmer and Gary Player.

Tee to green, Casper's play was rather dull, but with a putter in his hand he was an artist, the result of hours spent in the shade of the putting green as a young man rather than slogging his way around his local course in the hot Californian sun.

A winner on the US Tour for 15 consecutive seasons, Casper's other great gift was calmness on the course, stemming from his strong religious convictions. A Mormon and father to 11 children, Casper fulfilled a weighty promise after pulling off one of the sport's most incredible comebacks to win the 1966 US Open. Seven shots adrift of the apparently unstoppable Palmer with just the back nine to play, Casper clawed back the deficit and won an 18-hole play-off after promising to spread God's message if he took his second US Open title.

The unshakeable American is also a superb marksman and though his game was often underrated he was twice voted PGA player of the year and won the Vardon Trophy for the lowest stroke average

'If he couldn't putt, he'd be selling hot dogs behind the tee.'
Ben Hogan on Casper

Casper *factfile*

Born: 24.6.1931, San Diego, California
Country: USA
Major victories: 3 (US Open 1959, 1966, US Masters 1970)

28

Billy Casper pulled off one of the most astonishing comebacks in history when he won the 1966 US Open

over a season no fewer than five times. A stubborn competitor, in eight Ryder Cup appearances he lost only seven of 37 matches played and racked up more points than any other American.

Now an occasional participant on the US Senior Tour, Casper fills his time with course design projects and his commitments to God and 16 grandchildren.

Nick Price

'I've made $800,000 around the world. If people want to call that a "bad year", I'll take bad years from here on in.'

Price on his 1995 season

Born in South Africa, registered in Zimbabwe where he spent most of his youth, and holder of a British passport courtesy of his British parents, the gritty Nick Price is a leading contender for the title of player of the 1990s. A long-time star of the European Tour, he could and should have won the British Open as long ago as 1982 but was three over par for the last four holes and lost to Tom Watson by one.

Lesson learned, the Zimbabwean has seldom played poorly when in contention since and the only surprise was that it was a decade before he took a Major title. When he did, in the '92 US PGA, Price set off to the top of the world rankings and stayed there for three years.

Showing steely will and an unerring putter, Price won seven times in 1994 and became only the sixth man since the War to win back-to-back Majors. Still ranked in the world's top 10 after 23 pro seasons, the phlegmatic African will not readily give way to golf's new guard.

Price *factfile*

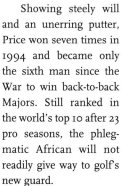

Born: 28.1.1957, Durban
Country: Zimbabwe
Major victories: 3
(British Open 1994,
US PGA 1992, 1994)

The Price was right in 1994 when the Zimbabwean won back-to-back Majors

Bobby Locke

'Old Muffin Face', as he was dubbed by the Americans, had the long game of a hacker and the short game of a golfing genius. Christened Arthur d'Arcy Locke but known as Bobby after his hero, Bobby Jones, the South

Locke played for England in the inaugural Canada (later World) Cup in 1953, but subsequently represented South Africa.

Locke *factfile*

Born: 20.11.1917, Germiston
Died: 1987
Country: South Africa
Major victories: 4 (British Open 1949, 1950, 1952, 1957)

Locke, above, on an early trip to Britain before the War and, left, winning the Open for the fourth time, in 1957

African played with a hook so pronounced that when he stood on the tee it seemed that he was playing a different hole from his companions. However, he was always confident of holing even his most wayward approaches.

After serving with distinction in the South African Air Force during the Second World War, Locke, whose other passion was playing the ukulele, headed to America where he was a regular winner, to the chagrin of some who resented a foreigner taking the glory. The relationship grew so strained that after winning the British Open in 1949 Locke was banned from the US Tour on a technicality and never returned, even after the ban was lifted.

Nearly always decked out in plus fours and his trademark white cap, the dour and deliberate Locke focused on the European Tour and events in his homeland, where he won the open title nine times.

did not deliver the Major his talents promised for several seasons. Instead, Olazabal was noted more for his Ryder Cup exploits with Ballesteros which made them probably the most formidable partnership ever seen. The two Spaniards brought the best out of each other: Seve passionate and pumped up, Olazabal calm and controlled, opposites attracting.

Just when Olazabal did achieve his move into the top rank with victory at the 1994 Masters, his career was left in ruins when he began to suffer with a foot injury so serious that eventually he could barely walk, let alone play a round of golf. Most of 1995 and all of 1996 were lost before the injury was finally diagnosed as a herniated disc in his back.

Underlining how much the injury held him back, Olazabal quietly returned to his best, winning the 1999 Masters despite the erratic nature of his driving. A measure of the Spaniard is that, after all the fuss that accompanied the climax to that year's Ryder Cup, Olazabal said that having a gaggle of exuberant Americans stampede over the green when he still had a putt to keep the match alive made no difference to his eventual miss, and that the Americans had been worthy winners. In just a few months the Spaniard had showed the increasingly corporate world of golf that there was a way to win and a way to lose.

Spanish style: Olazabal

Olazabal and Seve Ballesteros partnered each other 15 times in the Ryder Cup, winning 11, halving two and losing just two matches

Olazabal *factfile*

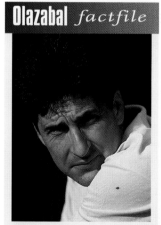

Born: 5.2.1966, Fuenterrabia
Country: Spain
Major victories: 2
(US Masters 1994, 1999)

Jose Maria Olazabal

Initially rather unimaginatively labelled 'the second Seve', 'Ollie' has carved his own niche in golfing lore, although like his more celebrated compatriot it has been primarily based on a peerless short game. A precocious talent as an amateur, the man from Spain's Basque Country quickly established himself as one of the leaders on the European Tour but

Babe Zaharias

A natural talent: Babe Zaharias excelled at every sport

'I just loosen my girdle and let it fly.'

The only golfer in the top 100 who would challenge for the title of 'Athlete of the Century', Mildred Ella Didrikson Zaharias was a true natural at everything she turned her hand to, winning the 80-metre hurdles and javelin titles at the 1932 Olympics, playing professional basketball and baseball, and eventually becoming the best golfer of her era.

Dubbed 'Babe' because her powerful baseball hitting drew comparisons with the great Babe Ruth, she took up golf as a teenager but was not able to give it her full attention until after the War, by which time she was already a sporting legend. Married to a Texas wrestler who managed her, she had her amateur status revoked because of her income from basketball and baseball, but was reinstated in 1946 and reeled off 14 successive victories, including the US and British amateur titles.

32

Immensely strong and supple, Zaharias was far more than a hitting machine, but it is for her power and flashy nature that she is best remembered. Arrogantly confident of her own ability on occasions, she was not popular among her rivals, especially as she pretty much cleaned up after turning pro in 1948, but her flamboyance certainly put women's golf on the sporting map.

Diagnosed with bowel cancer in 1953, her legendary status only increased when she returned to win the 1954 US Open. Sadly, the cancer returned and she died aged 41 having crammed several top-line sporting careers into one incredible life.

Zaharias *factfile*

Born: 26.6.1915, Port Arthur, Texas
Died: 1956
Country: USA
Major victories: 10 (US Open 1948, 1950, 1954, Titleholders Championship 1947, 1950, 1952, Western Open 1940, 1944, 1945, 1950)

33

Colin Montgomerie

*I*t is ironic that when Montgomerie appeared to be on the verge of his first Major triumph as player after player failed to match his score at the 1992 US Open, he should finally lose out to Tom Kite, then generally regarded as the finest player never to win a Major, for the Scot has picked up Kite's unwanted mantle. In 1999 he broke Seve Ballesteros's record of six European Order of Merit wins, and remarkably 'Monty' has won his seven titles in succession. But once again there was no Major.

Big, tall and powerful, the Scot's a natural talent who initially considered going into the business and management side of the sport after studying at the University of Houston on a golf scholarship. Never one to work hard on his game, he has been content to make do with what he has got, which is plenty. Never a risk-taker, he plays percentage golf, which is perhaps why he has fared best at the US Open and PGA events that favour consistency and accuracy instead of outrageous shot-making. If there is an obvious weakness it is a tendency to anger when things aren't going as well as he believes they should be. Though he has occasionally downplayed the fact he has not won a Major championship, asserting that golf has brought him all the titles and wealth he could ever ask for, great golfers are judged on their performances in the Majors.

He has been close several times, losing play-offs in the US Open and US PGA, but will it always be a case of 'close but no cigar'?

'My goal is still the same, to win a Major championship. I've got to get fit and improve my putting.'
Montgomerie at the end of the 1999 season

Monty is dominant in Europe after seven order of merit wins in a row

Montgomerie *factfile*

Born: 23.6.1963, Glasgow
Country: Scotland
Major victories: 0

Tommy Armour

The first and still the only British player to win the US PGA title, Armour was a pugnacious figure who lost an eye when his tank was hit by artillery fire in the First World War. Dubbed 'the Silver Scot' because of his prematurely greying hair, he emigrated to the US in the mid-1920s and subsequently became the only player ever to play representative golf both for and against the USA and Great Britain and Ireland teams, competing for Great Britain in 1921 in the competition that became the Walker Cup, then appearing for the US in 1926 in the competition that became the Ryder Cup.

Renowned for his slow play, in 1931 he completed a set of the three Major championships of that era, coming from five strokes back at Carnoustie to seal a popular win with the Scottish fans, who still regarded Armour as one of their own. Affected by the putting 'yips', Armour turned his attention to coaching, and was regarded as one of the game's leading instructors into the '50s.

Armour (left) completes the then set of Majors with a popular victory in the 1931 British Open at Carnoustie

Armour *factfile*

Born: 24.9.1895, Edinburgh
Died: 1968
Country: Scotland
Major victories: 3
(British Open 1931, US Open 1927, US PGA 1930)

Hale Irwin

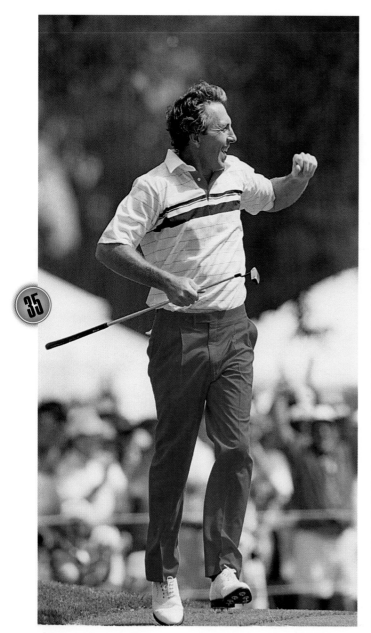

With his square-rimmed glasses and stern demeanour Irwin had the look of an accountant, and for a long time his game was about as inspiring as a visit to one. However, therein lie the qualities that made the former American football star at the University of Colorado such a tenacious and consistent performer, particularly on the tight courses prepared for the US Open. It was hard to see a weakness in his game, although he did not deliver the victories his considerable ability suggested he might.

A multiple winner of the World Match Play Championship at Wentworth but never a crowd favourite, Irwin is often remembered as the unfortunate player who casually leaned over his ball on the edge of the hole in the 1983 British Open and took an air shot. Not too serious a mistake in most cases, but Irwin went on to finish a shot behind winner Tom Watson and missed out on a play-off.

That miss certainly gained him some sympathy, but he finally won the crowds over when he holed a huge putt on the last green to make it into a play-off for the 1990 US Open and set off around the green high-fiving everyone in sight. That he went on to become, at 45, the oldest player ever to win the tournament only emphasised his new status as a crowd favourite. He carried that momentum on into the Senior Tour, where he is one of the top-ranked performers.

Irwin sets off on a celebratory jig after securing a play-off place at the 1990 US Open which he eventually won

Irwin once had to contemplate playing his ball from a spectator's bra, but a ruling gave him a free drop

Irwin *factfile*

Born: 3.6.1945, Joplin, Montana
Country: USA
Major victories: 3
(US Open 1974, 1979, 1990)

Tony Jacklin

Jacklin *factfile*

Born: 7.7.1944, Scunthorpe
Country: England
Major victories: 2 (British Open 1969, US Open 1970)

Cup of joy: Jacklin's great success as Europe's Ryder Cup captain helped him overcome his decline as a player

Having had nothing much to shout about since the days of Henry Cotton, British golf was looking for a new hero and he came from an unlikely background. The son of a lorry driver, Jacklin's first job was as a steelworker in his native Scunthorpe, but by the end of the 1960s he was the world's leading golfer and beginning an assault on the US Tour that would net him a seven-stroke win in the US Open.

Superb technique, the result of thousands of hours of practice, a strong nerve and an approachable nature made him a firm favourite with the fans, but that resounding US Open win was to be his last Major triumph.

The reason for the rapid decline? The brilliance and pure luck of Lee Trevino, who snatched a second Open win from Jacklin at Muirfield in 1972 with two outrageous holed pitches that left the Briton a wreck. There were still occasional wins, but Jacklin's confidence was shot. There was consolation later in his career as he took on

Jacklin got revenge on Trevino for the 1972 Open, captaining Europe to victory over the American's team in the 1985 Ryder Cup

the captain's role of the European Ryder Cup team and played a crucial role in plotting two wins and a draw over the US team, including a first victory on American soil. Finally fully retired, even from the Senior Tour, in 1999, Jacklin admits his love for competition evaporated, an unfortunate end to the career of a golfer who did so much to pick the sport out of the doldrums in Britain.

came back from missing the putt that handed the Cup to the Americans in 1991 and yet another case of the yips to win a second Masters title in '93. It was a victory made more special by the fact Langer three-putted only once in his four-shot win.

A committed Christian and family man, Langer's greatest ambition is to win the British Open and even at 42 it would be foolish to count against this ex-caddie responsible for popularising the game in his country.

Bernhard Langer

A character of typically German resolve, Langer has proved to be one of the most resilient and courageous of golfers, becoming one of the world's top players despite being badly hit three times by the yips, which would leave him shaking and unable to control putts of no more than a foot.

Langer tried an array of grips and clubs in an attempt to rid himself of the dreaded affliction and each time the tenacious German has been affected, he has fought his way back to the pinnacle of the sport. Indeed, if Langer's putting had remained anything like as consistent as his peerless iron play, he would surely have collected the titles to make him one of the all-time greats. A stalwart of the successful European Ryder Cup teams of the last 15 years, the methodical Langer

'No one could have holed that putt. The pressure was too great.'
Seve Ballesteros
on Langer's missed putt
at the 1991 Ryder Cup

Putting yourself together: Langer has suffered the yips three times and the trauma of his miss at Kiawah Island, right, but still fought back to win titles

Langer *factfile*

Born: 27.8.1957, Anhausen
Country: Germany
Major victories: 2 (US Masters 1985, 1993)

38

Jimmy Demaret

It says a lot for the outrageousness of his attire that Demaret is best known for the flamboyant extravagance of his wardrobe than for becoming the first man to win three Masters titles. In the sartorial stakes he was very much the successor to Walter Hagen. However, while Hagen never looked anything less than stylish, Demaret would often wear outfits that suggested a total lack of colour co-ordination, all topped off with a tam o'shanter and a personality to match.

Widely reckoned to spend more time shopping for clothes than hitting balls, Demaret was still an awesome competitor. His first Masters win completed a run of six successive tournament victories and he had a 100 per cent winning record in his three Ryder Cup appearances. Clothes and Masters titles aside, Demaret was also a superb shotmaker and one of the first to use a fade instead a draw, the shot favoured by most players then because the top spin on the ball meant it rolled more when it landed. Demaret, though, realised that using side spin with a fade he could get more control.

'The son of a bitch holed it.'
Demaret, who became a larger-than-life TV commentator, on seeing Lew Worsham hole a wedge shot to win a tournament

Jimmy Demaret had a style all his own

Demaret *factfile*

Born: 10.5.1910, Houston, Texas
Country: USA
Major victories: 3 (US Masters 1940, 1947, 1950)

Cary Middlecoff

39

could spend as long as a minute preparing to hit a shot, slow even by today's standards. During an 18-hole play-off for the 1957 US Open, his opponent, Dick Mayer, took a fold-up chair out on to the course to sit on while Middlecoff set himself up

After posting an early score Middlecoff took bets on not winning the 1949 US Open, and had to pay out when no one beat his total

in his ponderous way. Ultimately Mayer's waiting game paid off as he took the title by seven shots.

This reputation for plodding his way to success does Middlecoff some discredit because on his day – and there were plenty of them – he was capable of brilliance. His Masters title was won by an impressive seven shots over Ben Hogan, and Hogan was again the victim at the US Open in '56. Though he still won events after that, his nerves were finally getting the better of him and he retired in 1961 when the yips destroyed his confidence.

Middlecoff *factfile*

Born: 6.1.1921, Halls, Tennessee
Country: USA
Major victories: 3 (US Open 1949, 1956, US Masters 1955)

A qualified dentist unsurprisingly nicknamed 'Doc', Middlecoff was one of the dominant players of the 1950s, although he is perhaps better remembered as one of the most methodical and slowest professionals of all time. A nervous man, Middlecoff

Slow motion man: Cary 'Doc' Middlecoff, above in 1953, ground his way to three Major victories before he lost his confidence

Laura Davies

Standing 5ft 10in and frequently compared to huge-hitting John Daly, England's Laura Davies has reinvented the women's game over the past decade, blasting her way to titles all over the globe. A free spirit and risk-taker on and off the course, she admits having gambled away hundreds of thousands of pounds, drives a red Ferrari and has a football pitch in the grounds of her home.

An all-round sporting talent at school, Davies was told by her headmaster that there was no money in women's golf but has consistently proved him wrong, winning almost $1 million in 1996 alone. However, though she was expected to establish a Nicklaus-like grip on the US Women's Tour following her first Major success in 1987, her constant

'She's a player from another dimension.'
Ayako Okamato

Davies launches another big hit. Her style is to go for broke and damn the risks

Davies *factfile*

Born: 5.10.63, Coventry
Country: England
Major victories: 4 (US Open 1987, US PGA 1994, 1996, Du Maurier Classic 1996)

desire to go for broke and occasional frailty on the greens have sometimes been her downfall. However, her charisma and outstanding record have brought thousands of converts to the women's game.

Like Daly, Davies's power comes from a beefy frame, and the two players, who have partnered each other in mixed competitions, have much the same golfing philosophy: hit the hide off the ball and damn the risks. Not surprisingly, the crowds love this all-or-nothing attitude and galleries flock to see Davies strike drives more than 300 yards. Allied to a laid-back approach that means she rarely gets ruffled, Davies has stacked up the titles, twice topping the US money list despite refusing to commit herself fully to the US Tour.

Her success has helped open the door to other British and European players, and after years when they divided the spoils between themselves, the Americans now know they have some serious challengers.

Old Tom Morris

'Old Tom', as he was widely known, was golf's first great player, winning the British Open title four times in the championship's early years. He was also father of 'Young Tom', who took up his mantle and added another four titles to the family's roll of honour.

But Morris's legacy to the game was much more than his titles. Together with Allan Robertson, his boss in a club manufacturing business that overlooked the 18th green at St Andrews, Morris formed an invincible golfing partnership that remained undefeated until Robertson's death in 1859. To honour Robertson, a tournament was organised to find the 'champion' golfer, but though he was regarded as the favourite for the first 'Open' title Morris was beaten by Willie Park. However, their positions were reversed the following year. Remarkably, Morris played in every Open until 1896 and, at 46, is still the oldest player to win the title.

As well as becoming champion golfer, Morris played a key role in developing golf equipment, notably the gutta percha ball that superseded the feather ball. As the popularity of his 'gutty' increased, Morris also moved into course design and is best known for laying out nine holes of the famous links at Royal Dornoch.

Morris *factfile*

41

Born: 16.6.21, St Andrews
Died: 1908
Country: Scotland
Major victories: 4 (British Open 1861, 1862, 1864, 1867)

Champion player, club maker and course designer, Old Tom had a profound effect on early golf

Strange pretty much sums up the American's career. During the late 1980s he dominated the US Tour, finishing top of the money list three times and becoming the first player since Ben Hogan to win back-to-back US Opens. However, since that period of dominance Strange has almost sunk without trace, failing to fin-

Strange *factfile*

Born: 30.1.1955, Norfolk, Virginia
Country: USA
Major victories: 2
(US Open 1988, 1989)

Curtis Strange

ish in the top 40 of the money list in any season and not winning a single tournament.

As with many other golfers who have won Major tournaments and the riches that accompany them, Strange simply appears to have lost the desire that was so evident when he first topped the US money list in 1985. A pro since 1977, initially the Arnold Palmer golf scholar struggled, but a combination of superb long iron play and an unflappable temperament quickly began to

get Curtis noticed. In 1988 he became the first player ever to win more than a million dollars in a single season.

A great technician and with the ability to grind out a result,

Strange's identical twin, Allen, was also a pro on the US Tour

Sealed with a kiss: Strange celebrates his second US Open title

Strange was regarded as the Nick Faldo of the US Tour and it is ironic that his first US Open success came in an 18-hole play-off against the Englishman. His win the year after was easier, perhaps because with typical sportsman's superstition, he wore the same red shirt which accompanied his first title.

42

Payne Stewart

The storm that erupted over the 1999 Ryder Cup was put into perspective just a few weeks later when Payne Stewart was killed in a plane crash on his way to a tournament. The larger-than-life American, famed for outrageously garish clothes that always included a set of plus fours, had come out of the competition with his reputation as a gentleman enhanced when he gave Colin Montgomerie his birdie putt and with it the match at the last hole after the Scot had been subjected to abuse by sections of the partisan crowd.

Never a prolific winner, Stewart saved his best for the tournaments that mattered, twice finishing runner-up at the British Open and twice finishing second to Lee Janzen at the US Open. When only one tournament victory followed in seven seasons after his 1991 US Open title, it seemed he would be remembered more for his uncoordinated outfits that matched the colours of the local American football team each week than for his golfing talent. But at the 1999 US Open he was once

43

Several of Stewart's pro friends wore plus fours in the final round of the 1999 Tour Championship following his tragic death

Stewart *factfile*

Born: 30.1.1957, Springfield, Missouri
Died: 25.10.1999
Country: USA
Major victories: 3 (US Open 1991, 1999, US PGA 1989)

Plenty of pluses: With his garish clothes, Payne Stewart was always larger than life on the course and off

again at the forefront, pumping his arm in typical fashion as the putts dropped, whipping delirious galleries into a frenzy.

That victory gained him selection for the Ryder Cup team for the first time since 1993. The event was initially soured by a row among some American players over pay, but Stewart made clear he felt selection was an honour, and came through the competition with a dignity made all the more poignant by his untimely death.

Craig Wood

Wood was the Greg Norman of his era. Several times he seemed to have played himself into the history books with brilliant performances in Major championships, only for one of his rivals to sneak in at the death, usually in a play-off.

The most renowned upset in which Wood was involved, and in fact one of the most notable of all time, came in the 1935 Masters. With Amen Corner behind him Wood was well down the finishing stretch and holding a three-shot lead. Then Gene Sarazen holed his second shot for an albatross at the par-five 15th – later dubbed 'the shot heard around the world' – and went on to beat Wood in a play-off. Just like Norman, Wood completed an unfortunate quartet of Major defeats, a loss in the play-off for the 1939 US Open giving him an unhappy grand slam.

When Wood's moment finally did arrive and he clinched two Majors in 1941, the outbreak of war meant that the Tour effectively closed down for several years and with it went his winning streak.

> After the 1935 Masters, Wood was undone by another albatross in the play-off for 1939 US Open, Byron Nelson holing out on a par five and eventually winning by three

Wood *factfile*

Born: 11.10.1901, Lake Placid, New York
Country: USA
Major victories: 2
(US Masters 1941,
US Open 1941)

44

Thanks, lads: Wood and two of his biggest rivals, Denny Shute, centre, and Byron Nelson, who beat him in play-offs for the British Open and US Open titles respectively

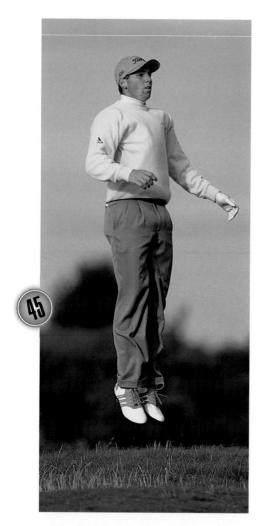

45

two European Tour events and then chasing Woods all the way to the post at the US PGA, where his good looks, beaming smile and outrageously flamboyant play won over the crowd, particularly the suddenly apparent young female element of it.

A worthy successor to Ballesteros and Olazabal, he has a superb all-round game and the youthful exuberance to get away with even the most extravagant shots, as witnessed by the shot of the 1999 season from the roots of a tree at the US PGA, which he sliced around the trunk and on to the green. From there he went on to the Ryder Cup and formed a memorable partnership with extrovert Swede Jesper Parnevik that almost anchored Europe to an unlikely victory.

Since he became club champion aged 12, Garcia has played the game as if it was the easiest task in the world. After making his first cut at a Tour event aged 14, winning the amateur medal at the 1999 Masters and charging into the top 25 of the world rankings by the end of the year, he probably thinks it is.

Sergio Garcia

*I*t takes an incredible talent to justify a place this high up the top 100 list after just a year as a pro, but, together with Tiger Woods, the young Spaniard is the future of golf. Nicknamed 'El Niño' (boy), Garcia made the most dramatic of entrances to the professional scene last season, winning

Garcia *factfile*

Born: 9.1.1980, Borriol
Country: Spain
Major victories: 0

'He's even, arguably, better than Tiger was at the same stage of his development.'
Colin Montgomerie

Blowing like a storm through the staid world of golf, 'El Niño' Garcia amazed many with his ability and maturity, and delighted many more with his exuberant celebrations

Willie Anderson

Anderson's closing 72 in the 1904 US Open was the first time anyone had equalled par in the event's history

*L*ike Tommy Armour, Anderson was a Scot who emigrated to the US and enjoyed his best form on the other side of the Atlantic, becoming the first and still only man to win three successive US Open titles.

After sailing to America in 1896, the 19-year-old Scot almost caused a sensation at the US Open the following year when he was denied victory by Joe Lloyd's eagle at the final hole, the only time the event has been won with an eagle. Anderson was at the forefront of efforts to improve the second-rate conditions that were offered to professionals in that era, and his success on the course and well-respected modesty off it helped to bring about changes for the better.

Also a four-time winner of the Western Open, then the other leading US tournament, the nerveless Scot died soon after playing an exhibition match, with alcohol said to be at the root of his premature demise.

Willie Anderson, an immigrant Scot, beat the Americans on their own turf, establishing a formidable US Open record

Anderson *factfile*

46

Born: 1880, North Berwick
Died: 1910
Country: Scotland
Major victories: 4
(US Open 1901, 1903, 1904, 1905)

47

Kathy Whitworth

In 1981 Kathy Whitworth became the first female
player to pass $1 million in career earnings

Though she did not achieve her ambition of
becoming the best woman player of all time, the
Texan did rack up more tournament wins than
any other woman and topped the money list eight years
in a row from 1965, a fair achievement for a player
whose swing can be best described as awkward.

A student of celebrated coach Harvey Penick, who
also worked with Tom Kite and Ben Crenshaw,
Whitworth's strengths were total consistency under
pressure, mental resilience and a gifted touch on the
greens. Her swing was no thing of beauty, but hours of
practice meant that it never let her down, although as a
young pro she was so diligent that it was pointed out she
was leaving all her best shots on the range.

As she was not blessed with the same natural ability
as the likes of Mickey Wright and Patty Berg, Whitworth
based her long-time supremacy on her course management, playing risk-free golf that kept her out of trouble
and always in the frame.

Miss Consistency: Whitworth topped the money list from '65 to '72

Whitworth *factfile*

Born: 27.9.1939, Monahans, Texas
Country: USA
Major victories: 6 (US LPGA 1967,
1971, 1975, Titleholders Championship
1965, 1966, Western Open 1967)

John Ball

*B*all is not one of the best remembered of the early golfing greats, but he deserves his place in history as both the first Englishman to win the British Open and as one of the best amateur players of all time. His eight British Amateur Championship wins are still a record and it can be argued that as the championship was then regarded as a Major, Ball is in fact the most successful European player of all time.

The son of a golfing father who owned the Royal Hotel at Hoylake, Ball tied for fourth at the British Open in 1878 when still a teenager but it was another decade before he took his first amateur title. Ball's long run of success can be put down to supreme iron play. Never a great putter, the Englishman was the first player to shoot directly for the flag rather than just aiming for the green. So accurate was his hitting that when dense fog descended on Hoylake one afternoon, Ball took on a wager that he would not be able to play a round with the same ball and shoot under 90. Little more than two hours later he was back with the same ball having played Hoylake 'blind' in 81 strokes.

Ball *factfile*

Born: 24.12.1861, Hoylake
Died: 1940
Country: England
Major victories: 1 (British Open 1890)

Iron man: Ball developed his iron play to a new level, shooting for the flag rather than just the green

48

Jim Barnes

Jim Barnes, a Cornishman living in America, completed his sweep of all the Majors then available when he won the British Open at Prestwick in 1925

Known as 'Long Jim' for his height (6ft 3in) and hitting, Barnes was born in Cornwall, emigrated to San Francisco in 1906 and enjoyed one of the longest professional careers in the sport's history. In 1937 he had his final win on the US Tour at the age of 51, a record that stood until broken by 52-year-old Sam Snead in 1965.

He completed a sweep of all the Major tournaments of the era in 1925 when he returned to Britain for his fourth attempt on the Open Championship. Barnes seemed well out of it as local fans descended in their thousands on Prestwick expecting to see Scot MacDonald Smith clinch the trophy. But Smith shot 82 as the crowds roamed unchecked around him and the Claret Jug went to Barnes. The winner

of the first two US PGA titles, which were separated by the Great War, Long Jim contested two further finals against Walter Hagen but lost them both. However, he did have three wins in the Western Open, then regarded in America as second in stature only to the US Open.

Barnes *factfile*

Born: 8.4.1886, Lelant
Died: 26.5.1966
Country: England
Major victories: 4
(British Open 1925, US Open 1921, US PGA 1916, 1919)

Sandy Lyle

In 1985 Lyle became the first home player to win the
British Open since Tony Jacklin in 1969

When Alexander Walter Lyle took his second victory in the Majors in 1988 and ended the year second in the world rankings it seemed that he and not Nick Faldo was set to become the most successful modern British golfer. In 1990 Seve Ballesteros still rated Lyle as by far the most talented player on the European Tour, but since his Masters triumph the amiable English-born Scot has struggled to get into contention anywhere, let alone win a Major.

Lyle's problem has been an attempt to follow Faldo's route of reworking his swing in order to remove the inconsistencies from his game. This has only succeeded in quelling the natural ability that took Lyle to his great successes in the first place. An imposing but very easygoing figure, when asked what

50

he thought about when he addressed the ball he replied: 'Hitting it.' Unfortunately, in recent seasons there seems to have been much more going through his mind.

When his confidence reached the same heights as his ability in the late 1980s Lyle was a threat everywhere he played. In 1988 he won three US Tour events, including the Masters, which he clinched with one of the best shots of all time. Needing a par to force a play-off with Mark Calcavecchia, Lyle drove into a fairway bunker, but hit a seven-iron so cleanly that it carried to the green and left him with a 10-foot putt which he holed for outright victory.

Lyle *factfile*

Born: 9.2.1958, Shrewsbury
Country: England
Major victories: 2 (British Open 1985, US Masters 1988)

Lyle's decline has been a sad sight after his previous outstanding successes in the Majors

Tom Weiskopf

*T*here are many tales of underachievement in golf, but Tom Weiskopf's is perhaps the most striking. Dubbed 'Terrible Tom' and 'The Towering Inferno' by the American press, the statuesque Weiskopf had the finest swing in recent golf history but never reached the heights his game suggested he should.

Peerless from tee to green, he was often let down by his putting, but when his game did all come right he was close to unbeatable. In 1973, motivated like never before by the death of his father, Weiskopf won five tournaments in two months, including the British Open, which he led from start to finish, becoming the first player to do so since Henry Cotton in 1934.

A Ryder Cup player in 1973 and '75, his decision to miss the 1977 tournament because he preferred to go on a hunting trip underlined that Weiskopf believed there was much more to life than golf. However, he is once again coming into his own within the sport, this time as a much sought-after designer, and his Loch Lomond layout in Scotland is recognised as one of the best new courses in the world.

Swinging back into fashion: Weiskopf never won the number of tournaments his talent suggested he would, but he is now an in-demand course designer

Weiskopf *factfile*

Born: 9.11.1942, Massillon, Ohio
Country: USA
Major victories: 1
(British Open 1973)

Weiskopf was runner-up four times at the Masters, a record
he shares with Jack Nicklaus and Ben Hogan

Though she has only two professional seasons under her belt, it is hard to avoid comparing Se Ri Pak with Tiger Woods in terms of both her instant impact on the game and ability to spread the sport to a new audience. Like Woods a Major winner at her first attempt, Pak caused a sensation in her homeland, which was swept by Pak-mania when she followed her LPGA win in 1998 by taking the US Open title the same year. Congratulations arrived from the Korean president and for a few weeks the economic gloom that had settled on the country was forgotten.

Initially coached by her father and later advised by the king of the coaching gurus, David Leadbetter, she rarely seems moved by anything going on around her on the course and admits that she does not get nervous. Playing in dark glasses, her face an impenetrable mask, it is hard to determine any emotion at all, but at times the pressure placed on her by her Korean fans and sponsors has taken its toll, and at the end of 1998 she was admitted to hospital with exhaustion.

Standing 5ft 7in, her game is based on long hitting, a finely grooved swing, aggressive approach play and superb putting. It has all been honed obsessively to perfection, and perhaps all that stands in her way is the interest of the Korean media and fans, for whom she is the country's No1 sporting icon.

Pak's 61 at the 1998 Jamie Farr Kroger Classic, which she won by nine shots, is the lowest round ever on the LPGA Tour

52

Pak *factfile*

Born: 28.9.1977, Daejon
Country: South Korea
Major victories: 2 (US Open 1998, US LPGA 1998)

At the head of the Pak: The Korean burst on to the scene by winning her first Major, the US LPGA , and followed it with the US Open, left

Se Ri Pak

53

An accountant turned golfer, Julius Boros, left in action in Los Angeles in 1956, could count three Major wins to his credit, including the '63 US Open at Brookline, below

Julius Boros

Boros claimed the US PGA title at the age of 48, the oldest winner ever of a Major championship

O ne of the best sand players of all time, Boros was once advised by Tommy Armour to 'aim for the bunkers and you might make it' when he had mis-hit a number of shots during a lesson with the celebrated instructor. In fact, Boros almost bypassed the game entirely such was his dedication to his accountancy career, but after turning pro at the age of 30 he began to make an impression almost immediately.

An unremarkable figure whose strength was his consistency and ability to get up and down in two around the greens, his peers underestimated him at their peril.

He saved his best for the tight US Open courses that most suited his game, finishing in the top 10 ten times and beating Arnold Palmer in his pomp in a play-off for the 1963 title. His Ryder Cup record underlines his longevity. He was 39 when he made his first appearance, 47 when he was selected for the fourth and last time, and of 16 matches he lost just three. In 1971 Boros moved on to the then small-time atmosphere of the Senior Tour, winning the PGA Senior title in '71 and '77, and in 1980 he was one of the six senior golfing statesmen who established the framework for the Senior Tour as we know it today.

Boros *factfile*

Born: 3.3.1920, Fairfield, Connecticut
Country: USA
Major victories: 3 (US Open 1952, 1963, US PGA 1968)

Willie Park Senior

Willie Park goes down in golfing history as the first ever winner of a Major championship, defeating his great rival 'Old Tom' Morris by two shots in The Open at Prestwick in Ayrshire. Park and Morris went on to dominate The Open during its initial years at Prestwick, but as well as making his mark in tournament play, Park was reported to be happy to take on all challengers in matches for money. However, so great was his talent that the Scot used to offer to play standing on one leg and using only one hand. Legend has it that even playing with this rather considerable handicap Park lost on only one occasion.

Like Old Tom, Park also had a son who was a leading player at the time and helped his father with course and equipment design. In fact, so closely entwined were the two families that Park and his brother Mungo were Tom Morris Junior's challenge opponents at North Berwick on the day that Young Tom received the tragic news that his wife had been taken fatally ill during childbirth.

Willie Park, the first winner of the Open, shows off the Championship belt

Park *factfile*

Born: 1833, Musselburgh
Died: 1903
Country: Scotland
Major victories: 4
(British Open 1860, 1863, 1866, 1875)

54

Roberto De Vicenzo

*O*ne of the sport's greatest ambassadors, the Argentinian Roberto de Vicenzo won more than 200 tournaments during a career that stretched for more than 30 years, including the national championships of 39 countries.

A true gentleman, he is best remembered for an incredible nine-month period when he first held off a charging Jack Nicklaus to win the British Open at Hoylake in 1967, in the process achieving his life-long ambition in his 19th appearance at The Open.

Then, at the Masters the following year, De Vicenzo was heading towards a remarkable success, or at least a shot at one, when he tied Bob Goalby for first place and preparations began for a play-off.

Unfortunately, De Vicenzo's playing partner, Tommy Aaron, had recorded a four instead of a three at the 17th and the Argentinian had signed his card without noticing, in the process confirming his four and unwittingly making one of the biggest, and most expensive, unforced errors in sporting history. A golfing legend in Latin America, De Vicenzo gained a measure of recompense when he won the first US Seniors Open in 1980.

'What a stupid I am.'
De Vicenzo after realising he had signed for the wrong score at the 1968 US Masters

South America's greatest player, De Vincenzo won the national championship of 39 countries and, in 1967, a Major, the British Open

De Vicenzo *factfile*

Born: 14.4.1923, Buenos Aires
Country: Argentina
Major victories: 1
(British Open 1967)

56

Lloyd Mangrum

Mangrum and Cary Middlecoff tied a tournament in 1949 after bad light stopped play at the 11th extra hole

Mangrum *factfile*

Born: 1.8.1914, Trenton, New Jersey
Country: USA
Major victories: 1 (US Open 1946)

The only golfer in the top 100 with more Purple Hearts to his credit than Major titles, Mangrum, who received his two honours for bravery while serving under General Patton at the Battle of the Bulge in 1944, recovered from the War at St Andrews and returned to the US Tour determined to make up for the lost years. He was runner-up at the 1940 Masters after shooting a record 64 in the first round, but he clinched an epic US Open in '46, going two play-off rounds with Byron Nelson and Vic Ghezzi before finally winning by a stroke.

Nerveless and daring, as you would expect from a much-decorated war hero, he might have repeated that success in 1950. It was one of the best US Opens and had gone to a three-man play-off between Mangrum, Ben Hogan and George Fazio. With Hogan a shot ahead on the 16th, Mangrum picked up his ball to clean off a stubborn insect and incurred a two-shot penalty that effectively sealed an emotional victory for Hogan, who had just returned to the game after his near-fatal car crash. In typical fashion, Mangrum shrugged off the incident. Though never again a Major winner, he was frequently in contention and topped the money list in 1951. If the War had not swallowed four of his best years he would undoubtedly have added to that one title.

Mangrum, above in the 1953 Ryder Cup, returned a hero from the War and went on to shine as a golfer

Ben Crenshaw

A collector of golf memorabilia and keen golf historian, 'Gentle Ben' burst on to the pro scene with a bang in 1973, winning his first tournament and on the back of a highly successful amateur career looked set to sweep up all the great prizes in golf, including the British Open title he has coveted more than any other. Occasionally brilliant but often mediocre from tee to green, the Texan is blessed with a super smooth putting stroke that ranks with the best.

A student of celebrated golf teacher Harvey Penick, who also worked with Tom Kite, Crenshaw considered giving up the game in 1982 after his worst year as a pro left his confidence in tatters, but he fought his way back to a second-place finish at the 1983 Masters, in which the wide open spaces of Augusta's fairways penalised his waywardness far less than at other Majors. Popular with galleries across the world because of his

'Ben is the best damn second- and third-placed finisher in the Majors the world will ever know.'
Anonymous rival

Crenshaw *factfile*

Born: 11.1.1952, Austin, Texas
Country: USA
Major victories: 2 (US Masters 1984, 1995)

graciousness and obvious love of the game, Crenshaw finally shook off his choker tag at Augusta the following season and scored an emotional repeat victory in 1995 just days after acting as a pallbearer at Penick's funeral.

He returned to prominence in 1999 as non-playing captain of the victorious American Ryder Cup team, and after the passion and controversy stirred up by the controversial and highly charged atmosphere admitted that the job had taken years off his life and that he would not wish it on anyone.

From Master to captain: Crenshaw, twice a winner at Augusta, skippered the US to Ryder Cup victory, right

57

Tom Kite

Still ranked in the top 10 money earners of all time, Kite will be making his first appearance on the US Senior Tour in 2000

B orn in Austin, Texas, a student of coach Harvey Penick, with a great short game and a roll of honour that hardly does justice to his talents. No, not Ben Crenshaw, but Tom Kite, he of the large glasses, Panama hat and strange, almost duck-like gait. A small, slight figure, Kite has a fearsome reputation on two counts: his short game is superlative – he was one of the first players to carry three wedges in his bag – and he never knows when he is beaten.

Unfortunately, these two characteristics have taken the amiable Kite to the verge of many Major triumphs but his relative lack of distance with woods and long irons has often left him short of ultimate victory. That Kite was more often than not in the frame is underlined by the fact that until passed by Greg Norman in 1995, the freckly redhead was the leading money winner of all time. Any questions about a fallible temperament can be dispelled by a glance at his Ryder Cup record. In a competition where you carry your own and your country's hopes, the Texan's tally is a mere nine matches lost out of 28 played.

Ironically for a man not known for his big hitting, when Kite did finally break his duck in the Majors at Pebble Beach in 1992 it was on a wild day when Colin Montgomerie posted a good early score and watched his rivals literally get blown away. But Kite has always performed well on links courses and held his game together to rid himself of the unwanted title of 'best player never to have won a Major'.

58

Joy at last: After many years trying, Tom Kite finally won a Major title when he fought through the wind to clinch the US Open in 1992, right

Kite *factfile*

Born: 9.12.1949, Austin, Texas
Country: USA
Major victories: 1 (US Open 1992)

Ian Woosnam

In eight Ryder Cup appearances Woosnam has never won a singles match

1990s. The camper has long since been forgotten and he now flies himself round the world in his own jet. However, his form recently has been patchy and led to him missing the Ryder Cup in 1999 for the first time since 1981. The question now is whether the determination that took him to the top can be rekindled to get him back there.

Welsh wonder: Ian Woosnam's famous celebration on winning the 1991 US Masters, below, has sadly not been seen at any other Majors since

Woosnam *factfile*

Born: 2.3.1958, Oswestry
Country: England
Major victories: 1
(US Masters 1991)

From camper van to private jet, the English-born Welshman's rise to the top is an example for any struggling pro of what can be achieved by combining talent with sheer guts.

Standing only 5ft 4in, Ian Woosnam is as tough as they come. He turned pro in 1976, but it was to be 15 years before the combative Welshman had scaled such heights that he was ranked No1 in the world. It took him three attempts to qualify for the Tour, and even then his earnings were so low he lived

out of that camper van. Brought up on a farm and a keen boxer during his schooldays, he is blessed with huge strength and a beautifully smooth and powerful swing that makes him one of the biggest hitters in the sport, and one of the most popular players among European fans.

The turning point for Woosnam came when he won the Swiss Open in 1982. He went on to establish himself as one of the new rank of European stars who swept up Major after Major during the 1980s and

*I*t seems that even being a friend of Tiger Woods can raise a player to greatness. How else to account for O'Meara's late blossoming? He had always been one of the most stylish players in the game, and at one time would certainly have been well up the list of the best players never to have claimed a Major.

The winner of events on five continents, O'Meara became good buddies with Woods and it seems that some of the youngster's drive and ambition infected his greying friend to the extent that after one summer of peerless play he was suddenly, and quite amazingly, the senior of the pair in

O'Meara has been deeply involved in fundraising to further research into multiple sclerosis after his long-time caddie, Donny Wanstall, was diagnosed with the disease

terms of Major wins. At 41 O'Meara won the Masters and the British Open and such was his form he tied for fourth at the US PGA and beat none other than Tiger to win the World Match Play.

One of the true ambassadors of the sport, O'Meara signalled long ago that he was one to watch, winning the 1979 US amateur title and two years later being selected as the US Tour's rookie of the year.

Titles followed, and in only two years since 1984 has he been out of the top 30 in the US, but his time for Major honours seemed to have passed. Winning the Masters at his 15th attempt was a lesson in patience, and following that up with the British Open to become the oldest man to win two Majors in a season showed he had more than a touch of Tiger about him.

Mark O'Meara

O'Meara *factfile*

Born: 13.1.1957, Goldsboro, North Carolina
Country: USA
Major victories: 2
(British Open 1998, US Masters 1998)

Mark O'Meara struck a blow for experience in 1998, sweeping to the US Masters and British Open titles in his annus mirabilis

60

Patty Berg

An all-round sporting talent who settled on golf as a teenager after a spell as a quarterback in a local American football team, Patty Berg is one of the game's greatest ambassadors. One of three co-founders of the women's pro tour organisation, the LPGA, she was America's leading amateur up to the Second World War and after serving as a lieutenant in the Marine Corps she set about becoming one of the dominant professional players, with backing from Wilson, the golf equipment manufacturer.

A feisty redhead with a good line in jokes and the ability to put across the fundamentals of the game, Berg toured the US giving golf clinics in between tournament play. Such was her ability as a shot-maker and strength as a character that Wilson would send its new recruits to her for on-course coaching followed by off-course training in etiquette and general conduct.

Her golfing heyday was in the 1950s, when she topped the money list three times and won the bulk of her 57 professional titles. Even after retiring as a pro, she continued to work as an ambassador for the women's game despite contracting cancer and being badly affected by back and hip problems. In 1978 the LPGA honoured her by establishing the Patty Berg Award for the woman who has made the greatest contribution to the sport during the year.

61

Born: 13.2.1918, Minneapolis, Mo

Country: USA

Major victories: 15 (US Open 1946, Titleholders Championship 1937, 1938, 1939, 1948, 1953, 1955, 1957, Western Open 1941, 1943, 1948, 1951, 1955, 1957, 1958)

The prolific Patty Berg at her peak in 1951

62

The American Ryder Cup team of 1965, left to right: Byron Nelson (non-playing captain), Tommy Jacobs, Billy Casper, Don January, Johnny Pott, Tony Lema, Ken Venturi, Dave Marr, Gene Littler, Julius Boros and Arnie Palmer

Gene Littler

'Gene the Machine' was blessed with a beautifully fluid swing and the all-round ability to make him a great champion, but after first winning on the US Tour as an amateur and then following up with a string of victories in the late 1950s, he settled for occasional rich pickings and fulfilling his love of classic cars. When Littler's rise to the top was confirmed with his 1961 US Open triumph it seemed that here was a player who would join Arnold Palmer and Jack Nicklaus at the summit of the sport. But Littler lacked the burning desire required to challenge consistently at these rarefied levels. He did go close to Major victories on several other occasions, but established a reputation as a player his rivals would most like to come up against in a play-off, losing 10 of the 14 he contested, including those at the 1970 Masters and the 1977 US PGA.

In early 1972 he was diagnosed with lymphatic cancer. Yet after treatment he returned to the Tour that autumn, took one of his 29 career wins the following season and fought his way into the Ryder Cup team in 1975 for his seventh appearance in the event.

> 'Here's a kid with the perfect swing, like Sam Snead's, only better.'
> Gene Sarazen

Littler *factfile*

Born: 21.7.1930, San Diego, California
Country: USA
Major victories: 1 (US Open 1961)

Having quit golf because of his lack of success, Ralph Guldahl returned to enjoy a period of mastery over his peers that ultimately ended as suddenly and unexpectedly as it had started.

Needing to hole a four-foot putt to force a play-off at the 1933 US Open, jitters on the green got the better of him, the putt was missed and he returned to Dallas

Guldahl *factfile*

Born: 22.11.1911, Dallas, Texas
Country: USA
Major victories: 3 (US Open 1937, 1938, US Masters 1939)

Guldahl once coached multi-millionaire recluse Howard Hughes by phone to a club tournament win, and received $10,000 for his advice

After a sudden retirement, Ralph Guldahl burst back into the professional ranks to claim three Majors in two years, only to disappear into obscurity again just as quickly

Ralph Guldahl

to nurse his ailing son. But after moving his family to California, Guldahl returned to the pro scene in 1936 backed by the Hollywood celebrities with whom he had taken to playing. It was a timely move because for the next five years his putting finally matched the excellence of the rest of his game. The '37 Masters slipped through his fingers, but at the US Open, while everyone was congratulating Sam Snead on victory, Guldahl posted a record total of 281 to win by two.

The title was retained in 1938 and the Masters at last followed in 1939, but by 1941 Guldahl's final slide had started and he slipped into retirement as a coach.

Isao Aoki

Nicknamed 'Tower' in his home country after the Tower of Tokyo, the 6ft Japanese is not exactly a giant but he is certainly the best player that golf-mad Japan has ever produced. Five times winner of their order of merit, Aoki was the first Japanese player to make an impact on the American and European Tours and during the late 1970s and 1980s was a regular and successful visitor to both.

His game is best described as individual. A former caddie who is totally self-taught, Aoki has an ugly swing that has more in common with woodcutting than golf, but really comes into his own on the greens with a style that is unique, eye-catching and often very effective:

Aoki *factfile*

Born: 31.8.1942, Abiko
Country: Japan
Major victories: 0

Aoki's only US Tour victory came at the Hawaiian Open when he holed a pitching wedge for an eagle on the final hole

bent over his hands, Aoki has the heel of the putter on the ground and the toe pointing upwards in the air at 45 degrees. When he first appeared at the British Open both the Aoki swing and his putting style came in for much ridicule, but the ever-smiling Japanese quickly won over the galleries who appreciated an immensely likeable personality who had worked out a golfing method that

64

Star of the East: Isao Aoki has come closest to being Japan's first Major winner

owed nothing at all to the textbooks. Surprisingly, Japan still has not produced a Major championship winner, but Aoki came closest when he pushed Jack Nicklaus right to the wire at the 1980 US Open. He also jointly holds the record for the lowest round in a Major championship after shooting 63 at Muirfield that same season.

Lee Janzen

Not many players can claim that a quarter of their career victories have been in Major championships, but that is the proud boast of the Florida-based American who has two US Opens among his eight US Tour wins. Rather like Andy North, who had two US Open wins out of three career victories, Janzen is a solid player who is deadly with a putter and quite clearly can hold his nerve in the tensest of situations. Strangely, the man to lose out on both occasions to Janzen was Payne Stewart, himself a two-time US Open winner, who was particularly disappointed to concede a five-shot lead to Janzen in 1998.

It was played at the Olympic Club, which had been made even tighter than the US Open norm, and Janzen closed with a 68 to produce the best comeback since Johnny Miller won the title in

65

Janzen's winning total of 272 at the 1993 US Open tied Jack Nicklaus's record for the lowest score for the tournament

Janzen *factfile*

Born: 28.8.1964, Austin, Minnesota
Country: USA
Major victories: 2
(US Open 1993, 1998)

Never a prolific winner on the US Tour, Janzen can claim to have shown his talents on the biggest stage, winning two US Opens in the 1990s

1973. Though he seems unlikely ever to set the sport alight, Janzen remains one of the most consistent players in the US and should he get himself into contention at another Major it would be foolish to bet against him.

During a career tragically shortened when he died in a plane crash, 'Champagne Tony' became one of the most popular players in the world, particularly among the press, who were treated to a drop of the fizzy stuff every time he won a tournament. Tall and good-looking, and blessed with a graceful swing and supreme

Lema's last British appearance saw him lose a seven-hole lead in 17 holes to Gary Player in the final of the World Match Play in 1965

touch on the greens, Lema treated journalists to plenty of happy afternoons, most famously at The Open at St Andrews.

Lema, who had never played on a links course before, arrived just the day before play started and did not have time for a full

Lema *factfile*

Born: 25.2.1934, Oakland, California
Died: 1966
Country: USA
Major victories: 1
(British Open 1964)

Tony Lema

Champagne Tony: Lema was generous in victory, and had the stylish swing to pull off a British Open win in 1964

practice round, but he did have the benefit of St Andrews' most famous caddie, Tip Anderson, as his bag man.

In the first round Anderson told Lema where to put the ball, the American put it there and scored 73. With a full round behind him, Lema then strolled elegantly away to a

five-stroke win that sealed a special place for him in the hearts of Scottish fans.

Defeated just once in 11 Ryder Cup matches, Lema would certainly have achieved a great deal more in the game but for his untimely demise when, bizarrely, his plane crashed on a golf course.

O'Connor *factfile*

Born: 21.12.1924, Galway
Country: Ireland
Major victories: 0

O'Connor made ten Ryder Cup appearances up to 1973, a record Nick Faldo surpassed only in '97

Christy O'Connor Senior

The best golfer ever to come out of Ireland and a huge character to boot, 'Wristy Christy's' record on paper may not stand comparison with other all-time greats, but it should be borne in mind that he rarely travelled to America to challenge for the three Majors held over there and on several occasions went very close to winning the British Open. Blessed with an abundance of natural talent, O'Connor had an unorthodox wristy action. Though successful, he did not earn anything approaching the salaries even of the top caddies today and the all-consuming target for him and his Tour colleagues was the British Open.

He finished in the top 10 on no fewer than ten occasions, his closest runs at the title coming in 1958 when he finished one shot out of a play-off won by Peter Thomson and 1965 when he finished runner-up as Thomson clinched his fifth Championship. O'Connor had 24 wins on the European Tour, where he was the top-ranked player in 1961. Still playing and scoring below his age, he remains one of Ireland's most popular sports personalities.

Making Irish eyes smile: 'Wristy Christy' was the dominant golfer from the emerald isle during the 1960s and 1970s

Harold Hilton

Based at the Royal Liverpool Club at Hoylake, where he won his second British Open, Hilton was one of the best amateur players of all time, yet he did not win the British amateur title until after he had won the British Open twice. A small but powerful man who chain-smoked his way round the golf course, Hilton often played in white plimsolls and was something of an eccentric.

The winner of the British amateur title in 1900 and 1901 when it and its American equivalent were still regarded as Majors, Hilton improved even on that significant feat when in 1911 he won the British and US amateur titles, becoming the first man to win both in the same year.

Later in 1911 Hilton was appointed editor of *Golf Monthly* magazine, although there was still time for him to win another British amateur title in 1913 between editing and course design duties.

68

Hilton won the first full four-round edition of the British Open in 1892, closing with scores of 72 and 74, which were unheard-of at the time

The plush Hilton: An amateur who won on both sides of the Atlantic, Harold Hilton also edited *Golf Monthly* magazine

Hilton *factfile*

Born: 12.1.1869, West Kirby
Died: 1942
Country: England
Major victories: 2 (British Open 1892, 1897)

Lawson Little

*P*icking up the mantle laid aside by Bobby Jones, Little became the pre-eminent amateur golfer of his era, so much so that for two years he was well nigh unbeatable. Having gone to Britain as a member of the 1934 US Walker Cup team and anchored them to victory, he stayed on for the amateur championship at Prestwick and crushed Scotland's J Wallace 14&13 in the final. He was hardly less impressive on his return home as he completed the amateur double. When he repeated the feat the following year, the obvious move was to turn professional.

Playing regularly against more golfers with better ability, Little was unable to show the same high level of consistency. He performed well at the Masters without looking set for a Green Jacket, but did make it into a play-off with Gene Sarazen at the US Open in 1940. Playing in the kind of head-to-head situation in which he thrived, Little defeated his much more illustrious opponent for the pick of his seven Tour wins.

Little big man: The American was a giant in the amateur ranks, but struggled to take his success on to the professional circuit

> Little remains the only player ever to complete successive British/US amateur championship doubles

69

Little *factfile*

Born: 23.6.1910, Newport, Rhode Island
Died: 1.2.1968
Country: USA
Major victories: 1 (US Open 1940)

Betsy King

A good Samaritan whose Christian beliefs have led to her involvement in a number of worthy causes, including bringing relief to orphaned Romanian children, Betsy King was the dominant player on the LPGA Tour for a decade from the mid-1980s.

The best amateur at the 1976 US Open, she turned professional the following season but could muster only a single victory over the next seven years. Despairing at her lack of success, in 1980 she put herself under the guidance of coaching guru Ed Oldfield, who proceeded to rebuild her game from top to bottom.

The process would have destroyed the confidence of most players, but by the end of the 1985 season King had rebounded so far that she was ranked No1 in the world and never looked back.

Coolness personified on the course, her best year was 1989 when six wins took her back to the No1 spot and brought her the first of back-to-back US Open titles. Then at the peak of her form, she added the LPGA title to her list in 1992, becoming the first woman to play all four rounds under 70, and as late as 1997 she showed she was still a force in the game when she collected her sixth Major title.

King *factfile*

Born: 13.8.1955, Reading, Pennsylvania
Country: USA
Major victories: 6
(US Open 1989, 1990, US LPGA 1992, Dinah Shore 1987, 1990, 1997)

Seeing stars: Betsy King, above, models the US team's typically understated outfit on her second Solheim Cup appearance in 1992 at Dalmahoy

In 1995 King became the first woman to cross the $5 million mark in career earnings

Fred Couples

*I*t is hard to believe that with his handsome all-American boyish looks Couples is now 40 and that his best days could well be behind him. Nicknamed 'Boom Boom' for the huge drives he powers away with a long and almost effortless swing, Couples is a firm favourite with galleries but has failed to live up to expectations, prompting the feeling that his attitude often matches his swing in terms of application.

Couples' initial step away from his under-achiever's tag came as a result of a heartbreaking singles loss in the 1989 Ryder Cup to Christy O'Connor Junior that the American believed cost his team the trophy. He reworked his game and strengthened his resolve to succeed. In this he was helped by Raymond Floyd, who took Couples under his wing at the 1991 Ryder Cup and provided the motivation he needed to become one of the cornerstones of the US

success. Couples went on to record in 1992 the Major victory he had threatened for a decade. Ironically, the man he pushed into second place was Floyd, his motivator just a few months earlier.

He finished the season on top of the US money list and the world rankings. But since then, he has dropped steadily down the list, partly because of serious back problems, and it remains to be seen whether he can once again ally attitude to swing to challenge golf's new generation.

71

Fred Couples and Davis Love III teamed up for a record fourth successive World Cup win in 1995

Couples *factfile*

Born: 3.10.59, Seattle, Washington
Country: USA
Major victories: 1 (US Masters 1992)

Boom Boom: I win

John Daly

72

*T*he huge rewards on offer to today's stars are always going to force some off the rails, but few have gone off quite so spectacularly as 'The Wild Thing'. Consistently ranked the longest driver on the US Tour, Daly can look back on a career littered with marriage break-ups (three at the last count) and problems associated with gambling and alcohol addictions.

The blond Californian is a sublime golfing talent and one of the most popular players among fans. His philosophy is simply 'grip it and rip it'. On the tee he winds himself so far round on his backswing that his club almost reaches the same plane as at address, then he launches it back through the ball for an

Opposite: The Wild Thing at the Vines Resort, 1996

average distance of 305 yards in 1999. The problem is controlling all that power, and Daly's name does not regularly figure high on the statistics for greens hit in regulation.

Despite the drink, gambling and wild tee shots, Daly's record places him in a select group of players who have won two different Majors before they were 30.

His PGA win was unexpected in as much as he was not even supposed to be at Crooked Stick in 1991, but got a late call as ninth reserve and played without even the chance to practise. Remarkably, the course suited his long game and his silky touch around the greens took him clear of the field. By the time he won the British Open in a play-off with Costantino Rocca four years later, Daly was playing sober for the first time in his career.

Unfortunately, in 1999 he was dropped by Callaway, his long-time club sponsor, after drink and gambling once again took hold.

Callaway paid off debts of more than $1 million when it signed Daly, hoping to help him recover from his addictions

Daly *factfile*

Born: 28.4.1966, Carmichael, California
Country: USA
Major victories: 2
(British Open 1995, US PGA 1991)

Allan Robertson

The father of professional golf and the first man to break 80 at St Andrews, Robertson has no Major wins to his credit simply because there were no Major tournaments when he was alive.

However, he is indirectly responsible for the British Open, as it was his death in 1859 that led to the tribute of a tournament being established to find the 'champion golfer' the following year. Robertson's claim to greatness comes from the challenge matches that were popular at the time, and legend has it that he was never beaten playing for money.

He ran an equipment manufacturing business in St Andrews and employed Old Tom Morris. The two men partnered each other to one success after another on the golf course but eventually fell out when Robertson refused to countenance the development and use of the gutta percha ball over the more expensive feathery ball on which his trade was based. Morris established his own shop, while his former boss saw his 100-year-old business crumble. Ironically, that first sub-80 on the Old Course was achieved with one of Morris's balls.

73

Robertson *factfile*

Born: 1815, St Andrews
Died: 1859
Country: Scotland
Major victories: 0

Father figure: Robertson played in a time before Majors but his legacy in the game will last for ever as the British Open was started in his honour in 1860

74

Hubert Green

Green *factfile*

Born: 28.12.1946, Birmingham, Alabama
Country: USA
Major victories: 2 (US Open 1977, US PGA 1985)

'I owe everything to golf. Where else could a guy with an IQ like mine make this much money?'

The best you could say about Green's swing is that it is unorthodox. The loops and twists on the backswing cannot be found in any instruction manual, but despite appearances he was one of the leading players of the 1970s. His toe-in-the-air style of putting simply added to his game's homemade look, though his touch on the greens was wonderful. Rookie of the year in 1971, he advanced rapidly through the pro ranks and went into the last round of the 1977 US Open as leader.

Evidently one female fan was not so keen on his march to the edge of greatness and he played under a death threat. Showing great character he played the last four holes in par to win by a stroke and joked that the would-be assassin was probably an ex-girlfriend. That year he also finished best of the rest at the British Open, 11 shots in the wake of the great duel fought between Watson and Nicklaus.

Green's focus switched more to his family and emerging course design business in the 1980s, though he did end Lee Trevino's bid for back-to-back US PGA wins. Now a leading light on the US Senior Tour, he works in course design with Fuzzy Zoeller.

Fuzzy Zoeller

75

There have been few more colourful figures in golf than Frank Urban 'Fuzzy' Zoeller, a player who keeps calm by whistling his way along the fairways and enjoying jokey banter with the galleries. Accused by some of not taking the game seriously enough, especially in his wild younger days, his record compares favourably with most and but for serious back problems that almost forced him into retirement in the mid-1980s he could have achieved so much more.

As it is, Zoeller has given a great deal to the game in terms of entertainment. At his peak he was one of the most popular personalities in the sport, instantly recognisable from his ever-present dark sunglasses, solid build and jaunty stride. He was a rookie winner of the US Masters, and was widely expected to be a one-hit wonder who would disappear without trace. But Zoeller has stubbornly stuck around, his streaky, almost Aoki-like putting style carrying him to occasional wins, and as recently as 1994 he placed fifth on the US money list.

Fuzzy stuff: Zoeller has proved a long-lasting talent on the US Tour despite his laidback appearance

Zoeller *factfile*

Born: 11.11.1951, New Albany, Indiana
Country: USA
Major victories: 2 (US Masters 1979, US Open 1984)

'I have never led the Tour in earnings, but I have many times in alcohol consumption.'

Bob Charles

76

New Zealander Bob Charles holds a unique place in golf history as the only man to win a Major title playing left-handed. In the same year as his British Open victory he also became the first left-hander to win on the US Tour. However, these achievements overshadow his more notable claim to golfing fame as the greatest putter the game has ever seen.

Tall and willowy, Charles is a right-hander in all he does except when it comes to sports requiring two hands, the legacy of receiving a set of clubs from his parents, who were both lefties. Never one for trying to hit the cover off the ball, his game was based on finesse, straight hitting and beautifully accurate

putting – he averaged just 30 putts a round for his British Open title. Though not a prolific winner, he did claim titles on five continents.

A health fanatic who remains an elegant player, he was more prolific when he joined the Senior Tour in 1986, more than doubling his tally of victories. His final ambition is to play in the 2004 New Zealand Open, 50 years after first winning the title.

In 1993 Charles won the Senior British Open 30 years after victory at Royal Lytham in the British Open

Charles *factfile*

Born: 14.3.1936, Carterton
Country: New Zealand
Major victories: 1
(British Open 1963)

Annika Sorenstam

The first player, male or female, to top both the US and European money lists in the same season, the Swede's simple goal every year is to improve, and since winning the All-American Collegiate title in 1991 she has done that in dramatic fashion.

Progress went pretty much to plan until 1995 when the hard-working Sorenstam soared to a new level, claiming a string of wins on both sides of the Atlantic, including her first Major. A meticulous planner, she still managed to find time to get married while rewriting the record books.

Focused and unflappable, her game is based on accuracy from tee to green, and only her consistency and determination are spectacular. A rare visitor to European tournaments these days, from 1995 she has

11

Sorenstam *factfile*

Born: 9.10.70, Stockholm
Country: Sweden
Major victories: 2
(US Open 1995, 1996)

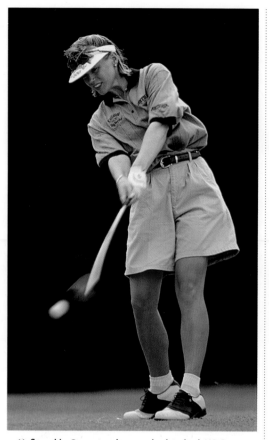

Unflappable: Sorenstam has won back-to-back US Opens

Annika's younger sister, Charlotta, also enjoyed a successful amateur career in the US and is also ranked in the world's top 50

been a fixture in the top three on the US money list, and although Karrie Webb and Se Ri Pak have recently stolen her thunder, you can be sure Sorenstam will be quietly working at getting herself back on top again.

Larry Nelson

78

A Vietnam veteran who did not even pick up a golf club until he was 21, Nelson is probably the best advert for the merits of instruction manuals there has ever been as he based his entire game on Ben Hogan's *The Five Fundamentals of Golf.* Equipped with Hogan's grip, swing and, apparently, his temperament and steely determination, Nelson broke 100 the first time he played and shot under 70 within nine months. Incredibly, he was playing on the

Eight of Nelson's 10 career wins were recorded in the south-eastern region of the US

Trophy-tastic: Nelson wins the US PGA in 1987, left

B est known as the man who holed the famous putt that handed the US its first Ryder Cup defeat for 28 years at The Belfry in 1985, Sam Torrance will captain Europe in 2001, stepping up from the assistant role he had under Mark James in 1999 at Brookline. The Ryder Cup must be Sam's favourite tournament – he has played in it no less than eight times.

One of golf's more easy-going and popular characters, Torrance turned pro aged just 16, helped by father, Bob, who is one of the leading coaches in the game. The English-based Scot's most consistent years were the 1980s, when he was a regular tournament winner in Europe and only fell out of Europe's top 20 once. Torrance, who is married to actress Suzanne Danielle, took his game to a new level in 1995 when he finally harnessed his abundant talent and pushed

Sam Torrance

Torrance *factfile*

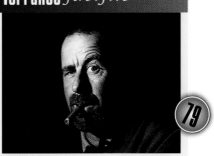

79

Born: 24.8.1953, Largs
Country: Scotland
Major victories: 0

professional tour by the age of 26, and although he has only 10 tournament victories to his credit, three of them were in Majors.

Very much a journeyman on the US Tour, his talent was being able to keep his head when all around his rivals were losing theirs. He went head to head with the then dominant figure of Tom Watson at the 1983 US Open and shot 132 for the final two rounds, a record for a Major tournament that still stands. This dogged determination made him a fearsome competitor in the Ryder Cup, notably in the victorious American teams of 1979 and 1981 when he had a 100 per cent record in nine matches played.

Nelson *factfile*

Born: 10.9.1947, Fort Payne, Alabama
Country: USA
Major victories: 3 (US Open 1983, US PGA 1981, 1987)

Sam celebrates sinking that putt at The Belfry in 1985

Colin Montgomerie all the way in the race for the European Order of Merit title. He won three of his 21 European titles in the process, and then played a key role in Europe's Ryder Cup victory at Oakhill.

Now inextricably associated with the growth in popularity of the broomhandle putter, which restored his confidence on the greens, Torrance holds the record for appearances in European tournaments, with no fewer than 624 to his credit at the start of the 2000 season. He was awarded the MBE in 1996.

80

Denny Shute

Shute *factfile*

Born: 25.10.1904, Cleveland, Ohio
Country: USA
Major victories: 3 (British Open 1933, US PGA 1936, 1937)

Oh Denny boy: Shute claims the 1937 US PGA at Pittsburgh

Vijay Singh

Aptly, Vijay means 'victory' in Hindi

O ne of the best US players of the 1930s, Shute first came to Britain for the 1933 Ryder Cup and left a few weeks later having made an indelible mark on the game. A determined battler, especially in the matchplay format that delivered two of his three Majors, Shute never made enough money from the game to be able to give up his job as a club pro.

Playing Syd Easterbrook in what turned out to be the decisive singles match of the

Shute was the last player to win back-to-back US PGA titles

1933 Ryder Cup, Shute came to the final green with a putt to win for the Americans. With his team captain, Walter Hagen, deep in conversation with Prince Edward, the Prince of Wales, rather than advising his man, Shute went for glory, went four feet past and missed the return, losing his match and the Cup. However, in what ranks as one of the largest turnarounds of fortune in the game, he moved on to St Andrews for the British Open, saw Easterbrook miss a putt to get into a play-off and then beat Craig Wood for the title.

P robably the only professional on any of the major tours to have held a club position in Borneo – and certainly the only man to have done that *and* won a Major championship – the 6ft 2in Fijian is one of the most dedicated players on the US PGA Tour. He was taught the game by his father, an aircraft technician, and modelled his swing on Tom Weiskopf's, recognised as one of the best the game has ever seen.

Unlike the naturally gifted Weiskopf, Singh has spent many thousands of hours perfecting his swing and even after a recent run of success that has taken him well into the top 10 on the world rankings he still works on his game at every opportunity. The only world-class golfer ever produced by Fiji, he played on the Asian, African and then the European tours, his long driving and good touch on the greens bringing him titles all over the world before he began to concentrate on the US Tour in 1993. He was their rookie

81

Practice makes perfect and Vijay Singh is the proof

Singh *factfile*

Born: 22.2.1963, Lautoka
Country: Fiji
Major victories: 1 (US PGA 1998)

of the year that season and all the hard work has continued to bring rewards.

Now based in Florida, his application remains second to none and it would be no surprise if he added a further Major to his 1998 US PGA win before too long.

Picard, right, and Byron Nelson had a famous duel at the 1939 US PGA, Picard winning at the 37th hole

Henry Picard

82

More famous for the assistance he gave two of golf's greats than for what he achieved himself, Picard could have won the inaugural Masters and during his best run of form in the late 1930s did secure the title, adding the US PGA the following season when he beat Byron Nelson at the 37th hole.

A smooth swinger who won plenty of tournaments but never played his best on the final day of the Majors, he helped Sam Snead cure his legendary hook by offering him his driver in 1937. Snead had always been fallible off the tee but suddenly he was transformed into the longest and straightest driver on the Tour and never looked back.

Picard's second good deed was to provide financial support for a young pro by the name of Ben Hogan. Like Snead, Hogan went on to carve his own considerable niche in golfing history. As for Picard, ill health forced him to reduce his tournament commitments, although he continued to play at the Masters every year until 1969.

Picard *factfile*

Born: 28.11.1907
Died: 1997
Country: USA
Major victories: 2
(US Masters 1938, US PGA 1939)

David Graham

A right-hander who spent the first two years of his golf career playing with an inherited set of left-handed clubs, the Australian David Graham led a globetrotting career in which he won titles across the world and established himself as one of his country's greats.

Work in a golf shop when he was 16 enabled him to trade in his left-handed clubs and he began a rapid rise through the amateur and pro ranks. Steady rather than extravagant or flashy in his wood and iron play, the nerveless Aussie came into his own on the greens and on his day looked like he would hole putts from anywhere, and often did. His tournament-winning round at the 1981 US Open encapsulated his strengths: on a course set up in typical fashion to reward accuracy from tee to green, Graham

83

Graham with the '74 World Match Play trophy

Graham is a member of the US Masters' Cup and Tee Committee that sets up the course at Augusta every year

Graham *factfile*

Born: 23.5.1946, Windsor
Country: Australia
Major victories: 2 (US Open 1981, US PGA 1979)

missed just one fairway all day and hit all but three greens in regulation – he still made the fringe on those three – to become the first Australian to win the title.

Now resident in Texas, he is one of the leading performers on the US Senior Tour and, like many of his peers, is heavily involved in course design.

Ray, Vardon and Jacklin are the only Britons to have won the British and US Opens

Ted Ray

A close friend of fellow Channel Islander Harry Vardon, Ray was unlucky to come up against the Great Triumvirate of Vardon, James Braid and JH Taylor at their peak, but had the game to steal two Majors from their all-conquering grip. He also played in arguably the most famous play-off in history when he and Vardon tied with unknown American amateur Francis Ouimet at the 1913 US Open. The British players were clear favourites, but Ouimet launched himself to celebrity status in America with an amazing victory.

A formidable man who wore a hat perched on the back of his head, smoked a pipe and gave the ball a huge clout, often almost toppling over in the process, Ray did not believe in holding anything back and was frequently wayward off the tee. For that reason he had a superb range of recovery shots. He did eventually win the US Open and Vardon was involved again, this time dropping several shots late on to gift the championship to his friend.

Ray's day: The Briton won The Open at Muirfield

Ray *factfile*

Born: 28.3.1877, Jersey
Died: 1943
Country: Britain
Major victories: 2 (British Open 1912, US Open 1920)

Winner of the inaugural US Masters, Smith's career was one of relatively unfulfilled promise given that he burst into the headlines by making it through to the semi-finals at the 1928 US PGA as a 20-year-old and followed that with eight wins out of nine pro starts in 1929. That he could not maintain that record is no surprise – who could? – but it was

Smith was unbeaten in three Ryder Cup appearances

Smith *factfile*

Born: 22.5.1908, Springfield, Massachusetts
Died: 15.10.1963
Country: USA
Major victories: 2 (US Masters 1934, 1936)

not expected that he would have to wait six years for his first Major.

It was an historic triumph because it came in the first Augusta National Invitational on the Augusta course designed by Bobby Jones and with Jones coming out of retirement to put his reputation to the test. It was fitting that if Jones was not to win, Smith, one of the few men to beat him at his peak in 1930, took the title. Two years later, in the midst of his best period of form since 1929, Smith took the title again.

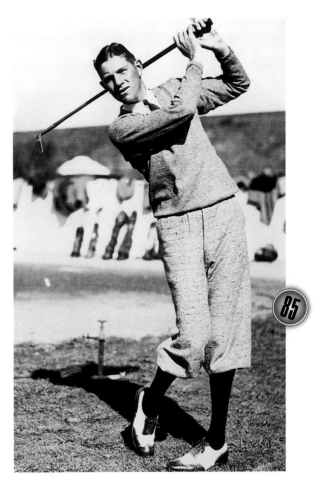

Horton Smith

The Master: Smith won the first event at Augusta

86

Lanny Wadkins

On the bounce: Wadkins won the '77 US PGA but lost the '95 Ryder Cup as captain

They call Lanny Wadkins 'The Streak' because he is either red hot or stone cold. Now set to be a contender for honours on the Senior Tour, the Virginian was renowned for blowing one of two ways. On his day he would attack every flag, his shots would come off and he would hole putt after putt. But when his awkward swing got out of its groove – and it often did – he would miss the cut by a street and be on the first plane home.

A fierce competitor who wore his emotions on his sleeve, Wadkins interspersed periods of brilliance – mainly in the late 1970s and mid-1980s – with years of near anonymity. An eight-time Ryder Cup selection who won 20 of his 34 matches, he was non-playing captain in 1995 and after selecting Curtis Strange as his 'wild card' saw him lose three matches and Europe win the trophy.

His US PGA victory is remarkable in that it was the first ever in a sudden death play-off, but it is perhaps even more remarkable that Wadkins' game did not get hot again at the right time so he could add to his Major tally.

Wadkins *factfile*

Born: 5.12.1949, Richmond, Virginia
Country: USA
Major victories: 1 (US PGA 1977)

'Put a pin the middle of a lake and Lanny will attack it.'
John Mahaffey

Only Peter Thomson has emulated Anderson and Young Tom Morris by winning three successive British Open titles

Jamie Anderson

Son of a caddie at St Andrews, Anderson was playing on the famous links by the age of 10 and became the second player to win three British Opens in succession after Young Tom Morris. Reputed to be the best iron player of his generation, in several ways his achievement was more worthy than Morris's because he won his titles on three courses following three different formats.

His first win at Musselburgh came over four rounds of nine holes; his second title at Prestwick – where JOF Morris, younger brother of Young Tom, was among his rivals – came after three thrilling rounds of 12 holes and included the tournament's first hole in one; and his third was on the Old Course at St Andrews after two rounds of 18.

87

Jamie Anderson, at his peak in the late 19th century, was an unrivalled iron player

Anderson *factfile*

Born: 1842, St Andrews
Died: 1912
Country: Scotland
Major victories: 3
(British Open 1877, 1878, 1879)

Johnny McDermott

In 1913 McDermott came up against the Britons Harry Vardon and Ted Ray, the best players of the day, in a challenge match and beat them out of sight

88

Hardly a familiar name to most fans of golf, McDermott could have been one of the all-time greats but for a series of tragic incidents that led to mental breakdowns and an extremely premature retirement from the sport.

McDermott practised obsessively on his local range, and shocked everyone when he entered the US Open aged 18 and finished runner-up after a play-off. Any thoughts of him being a flash in the pan were blown away when he won the title in a play-off the following year, becoming the first American-born winner, and then successfully defended it.

But then it all started to go wrong for the young prodigy. He lost all of his money on the stock market in 1913, then missed his start time for the 1914 British Open and had

Mac the strife: The American was a teenage prodigy, winning successive US Opens, but was forced into retirement in his 20s by a nervous disorder

to return home early. More disaster befell him when his ship sank, and though McDermott was rescued he suffered severely from shock and began to have blackouts and nervous disorders that forced him to retire in 1915. He never played competitively again.

McDermott *factfile*

Born: 1891, Philadelphia, Pennsylvania
Died: 1971
Country: USA
Major victories: 2 (US Open 1911, 1912)

Justin Leonard

Leonard *factfile*

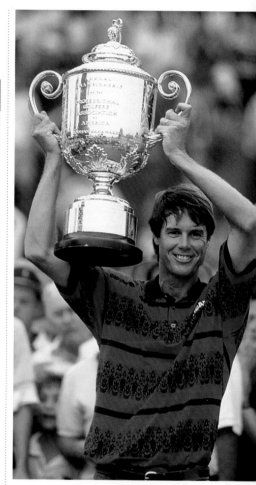

Born: 15.6.1972, Dallas, Texas
Country: USA
Major victories: 1
(British Open 1997)

Though he holed the putt that won the 1999 Ryder Cup, Leonard has yet to register a win in two appearances

Voted one of the world's most eligible bachelors in 1996, Leonard showed over the following four seasons that he has far more than just a pretty face and never more so than when he holed a monster putt that ultimately won the 1999 Ryder Cup for the US and had his team-mates dancing all over the 17th green.

So fastidious he has been accused of making lists of lists, Leonard brings this careful quality to his golf. There is no wild hitting and extravagant shot-making, just a good golfing brain plotting the best way to get him ahead of the rest. US amateur champion in 1992, he has a typically tough Texan nature and numbers fellow Texans Tom Kite and Ben Crenshaw among his mentors. Very close to his family, who take care of his travel arrangements, finances and public relations between them, Leonard has not been a big winner as a pro but unlike most of his contemporaries he has the ability to raise his game for the biggest tournaments and is usually in contention at the Majors, most notably at the '99 British Open which he lost in a play-off.

Very much the all-American boy with his good looks, manners and determination to succeed, Leonard has everything it takes to add more titles.

Having established himself as one of the top half-dozen players in the world, at the end of 1993 'Zinger' went to see his doctor about a troublesome lump on his right shoulder blade and was soon diagnosed with Hodgkin's disease, a curable form of cancer. The next year was a constant round of chemotherapy and radia-

Paul Azinger

Azinger wrote a best-selling book, 'Zinger', about his fight against cancer

tion treatments, but by the end of the 1994 season he made an emotional return to the US Tour and regular check-ups since have continued to give him the all-clear.

The tall and smooth-swinging Azinger made a name for himself when he pushed Nick Faldo all the way at the 1987 British Open only to bogey the final two holes and lose by a stroke. Rather than crumble, Azinger kept grafting and finished second on the US money list, his great wedge play and fabulous putting stroke always keeping him in contention. His best season was 1993, which culminated in a play-off victory over Greg Norman at the US PGA.

Since fighting his way back into tournament play after his battle with cancer, Azinger has struggled to regain his former lofty status, although he did have top 15 finishes at all three US Majors in 1998.

90

Corey Pavin

Azinger factfile

Born: 6.1.1960, Holyoke, Massachusetts
Country: USA
Major victories: 1 (US PGA 1993)

Few players better exemplify the phrase 'drive for show, putt for dough' than this slightly built Californian, who is regularly outdriven by his playing partners by 50 yards and more but has still managed to win and be in contention for many of the biggest tournaments on the calendar. With his Chaplinesque waddling gait, Pavin cuts

Pavin factfile

Born: 16.11.1959, Oxnard, California
Country: USA
Major victories: 1 (US Open 1995)

Pavin was outstanding in the early 1990s and joined the ranks of Major winners in '95 but has since been on the slide

91

an unlikely figure on the course, but for the first half of the 1990s there were few players more consistently successful or as hard to shake off.

Ranked No 1 on the US money list in 1991, Pavin's strength is getting up and down in two when within wedging distance of the green, and up until his US Open triumph there were few better in this crucial area. Since then Pavin's star has gradually waned and in the last three seasons he has not registered a single win.

Like so many others, it seems that having achieved the goal of a Major victory and financial security Pavin has focused more on his young family, and the result has been a gradual erosion of his ability around the greens that continues to leave him well off the pace.

Davis Love III

Tall, big hitting and possessing a beautiful touch on the greens, it is a mystery how this 6ft 3in American has just a single Major to his credit. One of the most consistently good players of the 1990s, Love's weakness is a mental one, although over the last few seasons he has been plagued by back problems that have occasionally forced him to pull out of events.

Son of a teaching and former tournament pro who was tragically killed in a plane crash in 1988, Love emerged on to the US Tour with a wonderfully rhythmic swing, a

92

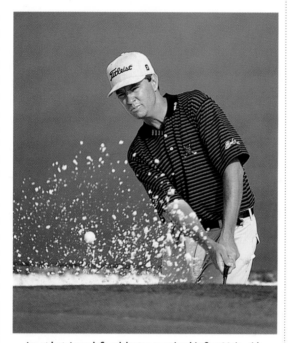

Joy at last: Love, left, celebrates securing his first Major title

legacy of his father's tuition. Understandably knocked back by his father's death, he has since become a regular winner but it was not until he beat his rivals out of sight at the 1997 US PGA at Winged Foot that he finally rid himself of his 'nearly man' tag.

A fierce competitor who counts on his brother, Mark, as his caddie, he has been selected for the last four Ryder Cup teams up to 1999, but his winning record is a surprisingly poor six matches out of 18.

Love's son, Davis Love IV, celebrated his seventh birthday in April

Love *factfile*

Born: 13.4.1964, Charlotte, North Carolina
Country: USA
Major victories: 1 (US PGA 1997)

Pat Bradley

Pat Bradley's mother rings a bell on her back porch every time her daughter wins a tournament and over the course of the last 25 years the neighbours must have grown very accustomed to their Sunday afternoons being disturbed. With 31 wins and more than $5 million in prize money to her credit, the hard-working and consistent Bradley has steadily collected titles and accolades.

Twice No 1 in the world, Bradley came closer than any other golfer in recent decades to completing a grand slam of Major tournaments. With the LPGA and Dinah Shore already in the bag in 1986, she went to the US Open with history staring her in the face and intense media pressure bearing down on her. She finished fifth. Victory at the subsequent du Maurier Classic and then the World Champ-

93

Bradley has finished among the top 20 money earners 20 times

Bradley *factfile*

Born: 24.3.1951, Westford, Massachusetts
Country: USA
Major victories: 6 (US Open 1981, US LPGA 1986, Dinah Shore 1986, du Maurier Classic 1980, 1985, 1986)

Tom Lehman

Six Majors, including three in one year in 1986, have helped Bradley to one of the best records in the game

ionship underlined the unprecedented vein of form Bradley was in.

She entered the Hall of Fame after clinching the necessary 30th victory in 1991, but with a new generation at the top it does not seem likely that the bell will be tolling again.

Lehman missed the cut at the 1998 British Open after injuring his shoulder doing a handstand for his children

A struggling pro for much of his career, Lehman credits his rise to the pinnacle of the game to his marriage to his wife, Melissa. So hard-up was Lehman in his early years that he gave up on the US Tour and played all over the world in the search for the cash that would keep his pro career going. Eventually he returned to the US to play on the Nike Tour, picked up a few wins and rejoined the PGA Tour far more confident in his own ability, and buoyed by his family and strong Christian beliefs.

Such has been his rise since then that for a week in 1997 he topped the world rankings on the back of his British Open success and an unmatched consistency. A hard-working pro who knows his strengths are his unparalleled ability to hit greens in regulation and excellent, and occasionally sensational, putting, he is as reliable as they come, a fact underlined by his great record at the US Open, where three years in succession he led

Lehman *factfile*

Born: 7.3.1959, Austin, Minnesota
Country: USA
Major victories: 1 (British Open 1996)

I've done it: Lehman wins The Open

going into the last round but each time failed to take the title. Added to a similar experience at the Masters, he seems to have a tendency to crumble when heading the pack. He did win his Open from the front, but his lead going into the final round was six strokes.

Though his best days are hopefully still ahead of him, Westwood merits his place in the top 100 as Britain's most exciting prospect and the player most likely to pick up the mantle of Nick Faldo and Sandy Lyle. A talented all-round sportsman as a teenager who was turned on to golf when his grandparents bought him a half set of clubs, he forced his way into the 1997 Ryder Cup team on the back of a series of exuberant performances that took him to third place in the order of merit.

Apparently nerveless in pressure situations, his relaxed attitude, confidence and good all-round game took him to even greater heights in 1998, bringing him victories all over the world, most notably in the USA. Initially affected by a shoulder injury in 1999, he came back to form at the US Masters and finished off the year runner-up to Colin Montgomerie in the order of merit. The next step up for the popular Worksop player would be to prevent Montgomerie stretching his domination of the order of merit to eight seasons, although he has the talent and seemingly the strength of character to surpass even that goal and add a Major title to his roll of honour.

Westwood is married to Laurae, sister of his fellow 1999 Ryder Cup player Andrew Coltart

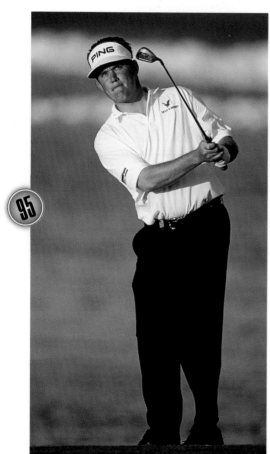

Lee Westwood, Britain's brightest prospect

Lee Westwood

Westwood *factfile*

Born: 24.4.1973, Worksop
Country: England
Major victories: 0

Son of US Senior Tour stalwart Bob Duval, the American, who wears sunglasses on the course because of an eye problem, has quickly established himself as one of the leading players in the world and has his focus firmly set on the Majors. It was five seasons before David Duval won his first

David Duval

Duval's event-clinching 59 at the 1999 Bob Hope Classic was the lowest final round in US PGA history

tournament as a professional, but then he reeled off two more in succession and has hardly stopped to catch his breath since.

He topped the US money list in 1998, led the world rankings for a spell in 1999 and in little more than two seasons has 11 US tournament wins to his credit. It is difficult to spot any obvious weakness in his game: his swing is smooth and reliable, his driving long, his irons accurate and his putting ranks among the best on the Tour. Perhaps the only criticism is that he has had a tendency to play himself out of contention in the third round at the Majors and plays his most spectacular golf coming from behind.

At the end of 1999 Duval took time out of golf to work on his overall fitness as part of his campaign for a Major. Certainly he looks the golfer best equipped to challenge Tiger Woods over the coming seasons.

Shades of success: Duval is aiming for a Major title

Duval *factfile*

Born: 9.11.1971, Jacksonville, Florida
Country: USA
Major victories: 0

Max Faulkner

Faulkner's victory came on the only occasion the British Open has been played in Northern Ireland

*I*n matters sartorial Faulkner was the forerunner to Payne Stewart, wearing plus fours and a splash of clashing colours, and keeping the galleries entertained. An ex-RAF man, Faulkner worked as assistant to Henry Cotton, and he followed him as a home winner of The Open.

In keeping with his unpredictability, Faulkner went to the 1951 championship at Royal Portrush with his game in a poor state. However, demonstrating his uncanny shot-making ability and finally showing some consistency with his putter, he romped clear of the field and despite faltering over the closing holes won what would be Britain's last Open title until Tony Jacklin's win in 1969. Faulkner's clubs were as outlandish he was. He shaped them himself and was always keen to try something new, especially different putters. But he was still one of the leading players of his day, winning 16 tournaments.

Max Faulkner in the Ryder Cup at Wentworth, 1959

Faulkner *factfile*

Born: 29.7.1916, Bexhill
Country: England
Major victories: 1 (British Open 1951)

96

97

98

Mickelson started hitting golf balls
at the age of just 18 months

Phil Mickelson

hander to win the US amateur title and, in 1991, the first amateur for seven seasons to win a pro event. Since he turned pro in 1992 the wins have kept coming.

His game is so similar to Charles's it is enough to make you wonder whether there is a benefit to playing left-handed, especially on the greens, where both are unnaturally gifted. A long hitter off the tee, Mickelson's golfing genius is most apparent on and around the greens, where he can manufacture shots that would not even occur to most other players. He has also been instrumental in popularising the lob wedge, which enables him to get the ball very high from around the green and stop it dead.

The big question with Mickelson is will he fulfil his potential by winning a Major. He has regularly been in contention, but played himself out of it, suggesting a mental block. But his talent insists that if he can break his duck, he just might win a handful of Majors.

Taking the Mick: The American has the talent to become the second left-handed Major winner

Mickelson *factfile*

Born: 16.6.1970, San Diego, California
Country: USA
Major victories: 0

Like Bob Charles, Mickelson is right-handed in all he does except on the golf course, and like the New Zealander he has the all-round game to make him a great champion, but still it has not happened for him. He learned the game by mirroring his father's swing, even though his father is right-handed. The switch has not held him back. He raced up the amateur ranks, ultimately becoming the first left-

Tommy Bolt

Combine a short fuse with the surname Bolt and you come up with the nickname 'Thunder', and this American never fell short in living up to it. When Bolt got riled, which was often, clubs would be bent across his knee or flung across the fairway. Caddies were abused, playing partners riled.

One of his most famous fits of temper occurred during the 1957 Ryder Cup when he

Bolt *factfile*

Born: 31.3.1918, Haworth, Oklahoma

Country: USA

Major victories: 1 (US Open 1958)

'Always throw your clubs ahead of you, that way you don't have to go back and pick them up.'

99

was pitted against Eric Brown in the singles. The American attempted to slow the quick-playing Brown by dawdling over his shots, but Brown responded by having a chair brought out while he waited for his turn. Bolt's temperature rose, Brown won 4&3, and Great Britain and Ireland took a rare victory.

Unlike John McEnroe, who used his temper to play better, Bolt would lose his composure and then the grip on his game, and could have achieved much more if he had been blessed with the temperament of Ben Hogan. As it is he won 14 tournaments in the US, notably the US Open in 1958, where he led from start to finish and never had to get upset with himself.

Thunder Bolt: The American was aptly nicknamed by his contemporaries, for his fiery temper often let him down on the course

Doug Sanders

'Sometimes I go several minutes without thinking about it.'
Sanders' reply when asked if he ever looked back on that putt at St Andrews

A player with a special place in the hearts of fans all over the world, Sanders was one of the leading golfers of the 1960s and one of the most flamboyant dressers of all, but is best remembered for the three-foot putt he missed at St Andrews that would have given him a one-shot victory over Jack Nicklaus in the 1970 Open. Every time TV shows Sanders anxiously crouched over the ball it seems this time he will make it, but it always slides to the right and the next clip is of Nicklaus hurling his putter into the air after winning the play-off and almost braining the cowering Sanders.

That miss would have been enough to give any golfer sleepless nights but unfortunately for the stylish – in swing rather than dress – Sanders it was his last chance for Major glory. He had been a perennial runner-up, losing out to Nicklaus again by a shot at the 1966 British Open, to Gene Littler by a shot after leading the 1961 US Open and to Bob Rosburg by a shot at the 1959 US PGA.

Still received sympathetically by galleries on the US Senior Tour, Sanders continues to stand out from his peers for his clothes, and still gets questioned about that putt.

100

Doug Sanders, a putt away from history

Sanders *factfile*

Born: 24.7.1933, Cedartown, Georgia

Country: USA

Major victories: 0

Since the 19th century, golf
has captured the hearts and
minds of millions the world
over and many great
champions have chipped
and putted their way to
sporting immortality.
Left: The much-missed
Payne Stewart at
Pebble Beach in 1991

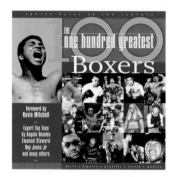

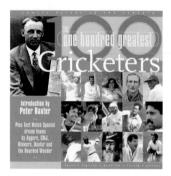

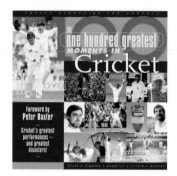

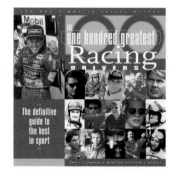

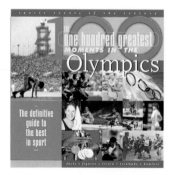

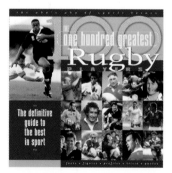

Available now from Generation Publications

(020 7403 0364)